D1199883

Elmwood
Endures

Hazel Dell Bridge in Elmwood Cemetery, 1889

Elmwood Endures

History of a Detroit Cemetery

Michael S. Franck

Wayne State University Press • Detroit

GREAT LAKES BOOKS

A complete listing of the books in this series can be found at the back of this volume.

Philip P. Mason, *Editor*
Department of History, Wayne State University

Dr. Charles K. Hyde, *Associate Editor*
Department of History, Wayne State University

Copyright © 1996 by Wayne State University Press, Detroit, Michigan 48201. All rights are reserved. No part of this book may be reproduced without formal permission.

Manufactured in the United States of America.

99 98 97 96   5 4 3 2 1

Library of Congress Cataloging-in-Publication Data

Franck, Michael S.
　　Elmwood endures : history of a Detroit cemetery / Michael S. Franck
　　　　p.　　cm. -- (Great Lakes books)
　　Includes bibliographical references and index.
　　ISBN 0-8143-2606-4 (alk. paper). -- ISBN 0-8143-2591-2 (pbk.　:
alk. paper)
　　　　1. Elmwood Cemetery (Detroit, Mich.)--History.　2. Detroit
(Mich.)--Biography.　I. Title　II.Series.
F574.D462E574　　1996
977.4'34--dc20
　　　　　　　　　　　　　　　　　　　　　　　　　96-11693

Design by ARCdesign Studios

To all of the Detroit pioneers, famous or unknown,
who are buried in Michigan's most historic cemetery.
This book is also dedicated to
Richard "Rick" P. Yonke, 1957–1993,
a true friend.

With thy rude plowshare, Death turn up the sod,
and spread the furrow from seed we sow;
This is the field and Acre of our God,
This is the place where human harvests grow.

—LONGFELLOW

Contents

Preface

Elmwood Cemetery, with its tall, brooding elm trees and regal mausoleums, is one of the oldest places of burial in Detroit. Less than two miles from downtown skyscrapers, the cemetery's archaic stone monuments are an artistic treasure.

The wandering visitor will find wildlife that nests on the banks of historic ground. Elmwood's stream known as Bloody Run was the site of an Indian uprising, pitting Chief Pontiac against the British Redcoats, in 1763.

Detroit's pioneers and warriors now sleep along those peaceful banks, dreaming of new frontiers and battling no more. Their names, etched in stone, have been given to parks, expressways, streets, and buildings.

This book chronicles the cemetery's history and its many occupants. The photographs provide a glimpse of Elmwood's spiritual, mysterious, and tranquil moods.

Acknowledgments

Elmwood Endures has evolved over the past two years and is really the collaborative effort of several people.

Arthur Woodford provided photographs taken at Elmwood Cemetery in 1889, and James Wilkie brought them back to life. William Clark worked arduously in the darkroom to develop the final touches on the photographs I have taken for this book. My brother, Mark, assisted me on several photo shoots regardless of weather or time of day and night. Joseph Malburg, the assistant manager at Elmwood, was a source of valuable information during the whole project. His recall of detail and dates still astounds me. To all of these people, I express my deep appreciation.

The suggestions and technical comments that helped shape this book in its final form came from Dr. Phil Mason of Wayne State University and Dr. John Dann of the University of Michigan. Both of these distinguished professors helped me rethink the presentation of Detroit's history and past burial practices.

Encouragement from my wife and devoted critic, Jeanette, helped me in the rewrite process and in the creation of a title that describes the essence of Elmwood Cemetery. A very talented writer, Dennis Ward, also assisted me in editing the original manuscript.

The detailed biographical information on the hundreds of people mentioned in this text would not be complete without the assistance of many librarians at the Detroit Public Library's Burton Collection and at the St. Clair Shores and Grosse Pointe public libraries.

Meeting Elmwood family descendants and civic organization members along the way during my research was an eternal reminder that Detroit's past survives into the present.

Finally, I am grateful to Chancey P. Miller, who has been the general manager at Elmwood Cemetery since 1990. With enthusiastic support, Chancey has worked with me from the beginning of this project. He helped me sift through documents, letters, century-old newspaper articles, local history books, and Elmwood's archives for the subjects and details in this book. His discussions and critical comments gave me insight into old burial grounds, a subject that has intrigued me since childhood.

Detroit's Memorial to the Past

ETROIT WAS HARDLY A SMALL TOWN when Elmwood Cemetery was founded in 1846. Vessels from Lake Erie brought new settlers to Michigan by the thousands during the 1830s and 1840s. As many as 2,610 passengers arrived from Buffalo in a single week. Many of them went no farther than the harbor at Detroit, which was still the state capital. More than half of its 20,000 citizens had made their way from New York, and many of the rest were from the New England states.

Main roads were a Hobson's choice between mud and dust. Jefferson Avenue was paved for a short distance with wooden blocks, predecessors of cobblestones.

Living was simple by modern standards, as described by Woodford and Woodford in *All Our Yesterdays*. Families, following religious beliefs, did not cook on Sundays. The city had twenty-seven dry goods stores, twenty-five grocery stores, eight drug stores, seven clothing stores, eight jewelry shops, four printing offices, and three bookstores. Other businesses included two daily newspapers, one triweekly, one semiweekly, and four weeklies. Professional services were rendered by thirty-seven lawyers and twenty-two doctors. There were no fewer than five private colleges and seminaries.

As Detroit grew, so did the need to make more room for the dead. Most who frequent the heart of the city today do not realize that they tread upon the dust of a forgotten population. Pioneer graveyards on small family farms were common two hundred years ago. Eventually, the remains in some of these graves were reinterred, but most were left behind in unmarked sites beneath public streets and buildings.

Before Elmwood

Records from St. Anne's Church state that on June 25, 1755, bodies were transferred from a burial spot to the churchyard inside the stockade at Fort Pontchartrain, then located on what is now Jefferson Avenue between Griswold and Shelby streets. This is probably the earliest known organized, Catholic burial spot in Detroit.

In the late 1700s, during British rule, another small burial place for English and Protestant residents was located just east of Woodward. A parking structure stands there now.

Before the arrival of Europeans, Native Americans also were buried near their villages in the area of downtown Detroit and Windsor. "They put sand over him" was what Indians said of a tribe member who had died. In subsequent years, pipe bowls, flints, and tomahawks surfaced during the construction of Woodbridge, Cass, and Griswold avenues. One Indian burial site, according to nineteenth-century historian Silas Farmer (who is buried in Elmwood), was where Tiger Stadium stands today. The Potawatomies deeded the entire farm to Robert Navarre on May 26, 1771: "We give this land forever that he may cultivate the same, light a fire thereon, and take care of our dead; and for surety of our word we have made our marks, supported by two branches of wampum."

Catherine Navarre is buried in Elmwood. Her white marble ledger clearly states that she died at the age of 86 on December 26, 1868, and that she was the daughter of Robert Navarre and Archange Messac (a lineal descendant of the duke of Vendome, brother of Henry IV of France) and wife of H. B. Brevoort.

Remains of the Indian village soon were forgotten as the farm passed from one generation to the next. Another landowner of that same farm was William Woodbridge, governor in 1840–41, who is also buried in Elmwood.

Two city cemeteries were established in the early nineteenth century before the founding of Elmwood and nearby Mt. Elliott Cemetery.

The first city cemetery was established when the Common Council bought two and a half acres from Antoine Beaubien for five hundred dollars in 1827. The burial ground was located between St. Antoine and Beaubien streets, one hundred feet south of Gratiot, where part of Greektown and Detroit's Police Headquarters are found today. Commonly referred to as Cemetery Lane, the burial ground was divided into two equal parts by a wooden fence, one side for Catholics and the other for Protestants. An entrance gate stood for twenty-five years near Jefferson Avenue.

Property from the Gouin farm, where Eastern Market's parking lot is today, was bought by Detroit Mayor Charles Trowbridge for the city's second cemetery in 1834.

Recordkeeping about Detroit's early burials was often careless and inaccurate. For this reason, the office of sexton was created in 1827 to supervise interments in the new city cemetery. The sexton's duties included keeping the grounds, recording the names of all persons who died in the city, the cause of death, and the name of the attending physician. As an old saying goes, "The doctor told the sexton, and the sexton tolled the bell." The sexton was paid fifty cents for each tolling. In 1878, with the completion of reinterments from the city cemeteries, the office of sexton was terminated.

The office of Wayne County coroner dates back to 1796, when Detroit was part of the Northwest Territory. After Detroit burned to the ground in 1805, the territorial marshall operated as coroner. Several years later, the position of county coroner was appointed by the territorial governor for a term of three years.

In cases of sudden death, the coroner could hold an inquest when examining the body. The coroner's fees were paid by the county auditor. For viewing a body, the coroner received three dollars. Ten cents was also allowed for each mile traveled to the place of death, twenty-five cents for each subpoena served on witnesses by the coroner to aid in determining the cause of death, and ten cents for administering the oath to each witness.

The Rural Cemetery Movement

With the onward stride of urbanization, both city cemeteries became inconvenient. They were too close to the city's activities, impediments to its progress.

Transmission of diseases also was becoming a public concern. Critics believed that rotting corpses exuded gases, commonly known as miasma, that caused various epidemics.

All the graves from Detroit's two cemeteries were finally moved to Elmwood, Mt. Elliott, or Woodmere Cemetery on the west side.

Elmwood's landscape was patterned after Mt. Auburn Cemetery in Cambridge, Massachusetts. Mt. Auburn was the first major cemetery in the United States not connected to a church, parish, or municipal entity. The cemetery was founded in 1831 by the Massachusetts Horticultural Society and New England's foremost botanist, Dr. James Bigelow. It became the model for the rural or "garden" cemetery movement—and also the paragon of the municipal park in cities across the United States. Because of the noted Americans buried there, Mt. Auburn was called the Westminster Abbey of America.

Bigelow, a physician as well as a botanist, maintained that Boston's church graveyards were a threat to public health. He proposed a design for a burial ground that introduced nature as a seasonal backdrop. Mt. Auburn's design was inspired by western Europe's first ornamental cemetery, Père Lachaise in Paris, which was founded by decree of Napoleon Bonaparte in 1804.

Père Lachaise captivated the French bourgeoisie. It was located on the former estate of Francois d'Aix de La Chaise, who was Louis XIV's confessor and an avid gardener. The cemetery became a favorite spot for Parisians to view great works of sculpture honoring local families of the past. It remains a major attraction today as the resting place of many luminaries, including celebrated writers and musicians.

Elmwood's Beginnings

When the pasture on the Baker farm on Detroit's Grand River was divided up in the spring of 1846, the building lots sold quickly. A subscription drive for funding of a new cemetery was held. Prominent citizens of the community paid $1,858 for forty-two acres of the George Hunt farm, which was described as being in Hamtramck township, two miles from town, and adjacent to Mt. Elliott Cemetery. Records show that the purchase was not a cash transaction. Interest brought the actual cost up to a total of $2,065.66 or slightly more than $44 an acre.

Following the dedication of Elmwood on October 8, 1846, eighty-two subscribers chose lots at an auction. Prices ranged from $25 to $100 (the higher end to be paid through four installments). The money was used to form an organization, purchase property, and still have funds left in the bank for labor and materials. Lots varied in size from 15 by 20 feet to 20 by 30 feet, with six graves to a lot. Subscribers who later did not want lots at Elmwood had their subscriptions refunded.

From time to time, funds from the sale of lots were used to buy more land from the Hunt farm. Land was also purchased from a neighboring farmer, D. C. Whitwood, bringing Elmwood to its present eighty-six acres.

By Special Act 62 of the Laws of Michigan on March 5, 1849, Elmwood Cemetery was incorporated as a nonprofit institution to be held in the names of six trustees: Alexander Fraser, John Owen, Charles Trowbridge, Henry Ledyard, Israel Coe, and John Jenness—all prominent businessmen and respected members of the community. Provided in this act was that all money received from the sale of lots over and above the cost of the ground was to be devoted to the overall improvement of Elmwood.

In 1850, half an acre in Elmwood's southeast corner was purchased outright by Temple Beth El, a Jewish congregation, and established as a distinctly separate cemetery. Today, this cemetery, now completely filled, is the oldest Jewish cemetery in Michigan.

A large sandstone monument was erected in 1852 in the area designated as Strangers Ground. Plots there were for the homeless or transients who could not afford to pay for their own graves. Throughout America, this part of a rural cemetery was commonly referred to as Potter's Field, the name used in the Book of Matthew (23:7) for a place of burial for the indigent.

Autumn was in the air when the first burial took place at Elmwood on September 10, 1846, three weeks before the grounds were officially dedicated. The body of Frederick D. Canfield, a grandson of former Michigan Territorial Governor Lewis Cass and nephew of Henry Ledyard (an original cemetery trustee), was lowered several feet into a small grave overlooking Chief Pontiac Valley. The cost of burial was one dollar. A month later, the Canfield family bought the nearby gravesites on the $100 lot at Elmwood's auction.

Frederick Canfield was one of thirty-seven infants buried during the first year Elmwood opened its gates. Of the forty-three adults buried that year, the average life span was thirty-nine years and seven months. This was noted in the original burial records still stored in the vault at the cemetery's 125-year-old gatehouse. Delicate, worn pages from Elmwood's registers provide vivid accounts of mortality in the last century. Each page within its crumbled binding is an inventory of causes of death. Today, most of the diseases blamed can be cured easily by modern medicine. The list includes typhoid fever, apoplexy, fits, old age, dysentery, dropsy of the chest, enpipectus, smallpox, rupture of the blood vessel, inflammation of the stomach, convulsion, congestion of the bowels, inflammation of the bowels, consumption (tuberculosis), phthisis, disease of the brain, bilious fever, scarlet fever, cholera, diphtheria, dropsy of the brain, paralysis, congestive fever, disease of the throat, disease of the heart, decay at age seventy-seven, scratch of a nail, and whooping cough.

Consumption, or "white death," was a common cause recorded in cemetery registers across the country. Tuberculosis was so epidemic that five out of every thousand Americans lost their lives to this single, dreaded disease.

Museum of Memorials

At Elmwood, behind every marker lies a story waiting to be told. Epitaphs not only provide factual data about dates of birth and death, but they also often narrate the spirit and the hardships of Michigan's early settlers. Many deaths recorded on the oldest tombstones in Elmwood date back to the summer of 1832. That was the summer Michigan's frontier turned host to a deadly newcomer.

On July 4, 1832, a ship en route to Chicago, carrying soldiers to fight against the Blackhawk uprising, docked near Belle Isle. Some of the soldiers went ashore and carried with them the intestinal disease of cholera, also known as Asiatic cholera. By morning, eleven people were dead. The ship was sent away, but Detroit had already been infected. Days later, the steamboat *Henry Clay* landed at Fort Gratiot (now

Port Huron). The disease was spread further when scared soldiers fled into the woods near the road that connected Detroit and Port Huron. Bodies found later had been ravaged by wolves. Others were seen propped against trees with empty bottles that had consoled them in their last moments.

Within two weeks, twenty-eight people died in Detroit, including Father Gabriel Richard, a founder of the University of Michigan, and Elizabeth Cass, the daughter of Secretary of War Lewis Cass. Two years later, the disease spread again, killing more Detroiters, including Michigan Territorial Governor George B. Porter, who is buried in Elmwood.

Thousands of markers in Elmwood testify to the brevity of life in the last century. The simple graves of children from the Protestant Orphans Asylum tell the sad story on their forlorn markers.

Quaint images are symbols of love, hope, or at least a fond memory of a life ended in its tender years. The lamb of sacrifice and the dove of hope are outlined on marble headstones. A verse from Longfellow tells the story as an angel ascends to heaven:

> *O! Not in cruelty, not in wrath,*
> *The reaper came that day:*
> *'Twas an angel visited the green earth*
> *And took the flowers away.*

A branch of lilac or blossoms from a horse chestnut tree once covered the tiny mounds.

Sheltered by snow, the monument of a small boy lies cuddled in childish slumber (photo 71). Sorrow shadows his mother's nearby marker. Once torn from her little ones, she is joined with them in words more lasting than death itself:

> *"Children?"*
> *"What?"*
> *"Mother Comes."*

In Elmwood, a small lamb is the most common marker for a child's grave. Its meaning—the passing of innocents—is as appropriate for such a grave as the trunk of an oak tree with severed limbs is for the grave of an adult. A tree monument symbolizes the manner in which death cuts off the limbs of the family tree. Small statues depict the individuality of the young hearts buried in Elmwood. A stare of wispy contentment endures on the face of Alice L. Dean (photo 16). Cruelly, the statue commemorating her life in stone is now disfigured, its upheld hands missing. Scarlet fever ended Alice's life at the age of eleven. More than a century has passed, but the statue continues to gaze downward at a burial spot that cost her family three dollars in 1884.

Cemeteries in Detroit became a regular business with the founding of Elmwood and next-door Mt. Elliott (in 1841). Rivals followed: Trinity Lutheran (1868), Woodmere (1869), Mt. Olivet (1888), Forest Lawn (1892), Woodlawn (1896), Roseland Park (1904), Grand Lawn (1908), and White Chapel (1925). Postmortem arrangements became commercialized and ritualized.

Mourning was a spiritual family and civic outing, with the funeral as the center of the production. Monument dealers and funeral furnishers were well established in Detroit by the 1840s. Catalogues in the dealer's office provided a selection of markers and memorials in all price ranges. Many epitaphs seen in Elmwood today were chosen from books that contained verses for every situation and condition, including about-to-be-deceased.

Materials used in Elmwood's nineteenth-century funerary art include marble, different colors of granite, sandstone, brownstone, bronze, slate, and copper. Most of the marble and granite used for cemetery markers in the last century (and in this century as well) were quarried from Vermont. Depending on the circumstances and the size of the quarried stone, horsedrawn carriages, ships, or rails were used to deliver the material to a stone-cutting firm. Once the marker or statue was completed, it was delivered to the local monument dealer. Many sizes and shapes were available, depending on the family's needs and pocketbook. All of the female allegorical statues in Elmwood were cut and chiseled by hand, some from Europe or states on the East Coast. An austere but comforting presence is sensed in their watchful eyes. Their expressions of melancholy, mourning, faith, and hope reflect Victorian attitudes toward hope of resurrection.

Many of the well-to-do families buried in Elmwood went to great lengths to be remembered by future generations. The obelisk that bears Senator Zachariah Chandler's name on the hillside next to Elmwood Chapel is forty feet high. Chandler's monument, the tallest in Elmwood, was erected in the early 1880s by a crew working a series of

CARDONI MONUMENTAL WORKS,

FRANK A. CARDONI, Sculptor.

IMPORTER AND DEALER IN

MARBLE AND GRANITE

Monuments and Tablets

FOREIGN AND DOMESTIC.

Cardoni's Gallery of Statuary, Statuettes, Busts, Garden Statues in
Marble, Alabaster, Bronze and Terra Cotta.

I also keep a full assortment of Designs, and anything selected from them I will
import to order on short notice.

SCULPTURE STUDIO, FLORENCE, ITALY.

No. 22 Gratiot Avenue,

DETROIT, MICH.

R. BRONSON,

UNDERTAKER.

259 Woodward Avenue,

DETROIT, - - - MICH.

lifts and pulleys. A fifteen-foot concrete base supports the four-ton monument. One can just imagine the size of the horsedrawn wagon necessary to pull the monument through the streets of Detroit, past the cemetery's gatehouse, and along the gravel road that ascends the hill.

Local slate was quarried by Michigan's early pioneers, a few examples of which are found in Elmwood. One marker belongs to Nathaniel Hickok, who died of cholera in 1832 and reposes in Section L. Another was donated by Chippewa Tribe No. 4 and belongs to Henry Freund,

F. G. MARSHALL,

Undertaker & Practical Embalmer

125 GRATIOT AVENUE,

DETROIT, - - - MICH.

(Telephone No. 1058.)

NATIONAL WIRE AND IRON CO.

COR. 4TH AND CONGRESS STS., DETROIT, MICH.

Iron Chairs and Settees.

Patent Reservoir Vases.

WIRE AND IRON GRAVE GUARDS,

LAWN FURNITURE OF EVERY KIND.

an Indian scout who died in 1872. A tomahawk and war club surmount his slate marker, which lies flush in Strangers Ground.

Elmwood's oldest marble slabs and ledgers are in Section A. One belongs to Colonel Elijah Brush, who drew up the articles of surrender when Detroit capitulated to the British during the War of 1812. These graves were reinterred long ago.

Here one also can see a few of the chest tombs in the cemetery. A chest tomb was created when the ledger was raised on legs and

EXCELSIOR
Marble and Granite
WORKS,

Woodmere, Wayne Co. Mich.

J. S. KENA, SCULPTOR AND DESIGNER,

Special Attention Given to Cemetery Work.

I will not be Undersold or Excelled in DESIGN or FINISH.

LATIMER'S
COACH AND COUPE BARN
Nos. 14 and 16 STATE STREET.

BAGGAGE WAGONS TO BE HAD AT ALL HOURS
Telephone Call 571.

COUPE SERVICE.
BETWEEN 7 A. M. AND 11 P. M.

FOR OUTSIDE CITY USE—Rate per Hour, ...$1.00
FOR CITY USE—Rate per Hour, ...75 cents.
No charge less than 50 cents.

BETWEEN 11 P. M. AND 7 A. M.

FOR OUTSIDE OR CITY USE—Rate per Hour, ...$1.00

COACH SERVICE.

For first Hour, ...$2.00
For each following Hour, ...1.00
Special Rates for Funerals.

enclosed on all four sides. Many visitors do not realize that chest tombs are ornaments, and hollow. The actual remains lie several feet underground. After damage from a storm or vandalism, the curious, thinking the chest tomb a tomb itself, might expect a coffin or skeleton. If so, they will be somewhat disappointed.

The more unusual the monument, the longer the memory of the individual. One of the more peculiar but often overlooked memorials in Elmwood is the copper-plated airplane propeller nestled in a blan-

S. ELSEY,

Manufacturer and Dealer in

HEADSTONES, MANTLE PIECES,
TABLE TOPS, TILING OF ALL KINDS, &c.

Also, American and Imported Marbles,
Freestone, American and Scotch
Granite, Etc.

422 and 424 St. Antoine Street,   DETROIT, MICH.

REFERENCES BY PERMISSION:

G. F. HINCHMAN.   MRS. JOHN J. BAGLEY.   THOMAS W. PALMER.
          ALEX. CHAPATON.   MRS. M. C. HIGGINS.

☞ Sole Agent for Michigan for the celebrated Hurricane Island Granite. Estimates on Monuments, etc., promptly attended to.

P. BLAKE.   W. F. BLAKE.

P. BLAKE & SON,

Funeral Furnishers

No. 17 ABBOTT STREET,

DETROIT,   MICH.

ket of ivy on the grave of First Lieutenant Alfred Brush Ford. The World War II pilot was shot down in combat over Ascheberg, Germany, on February 22, 1945.

No two monuments in Elmwood are the same. Many have become Detroit's historic treasures; Elmwood is a kind of art museum without walls. Decorations include both secular and sacred symbols. Ornament may be civic, fraternal, social, professional, heraldic, historic, military, or religious.

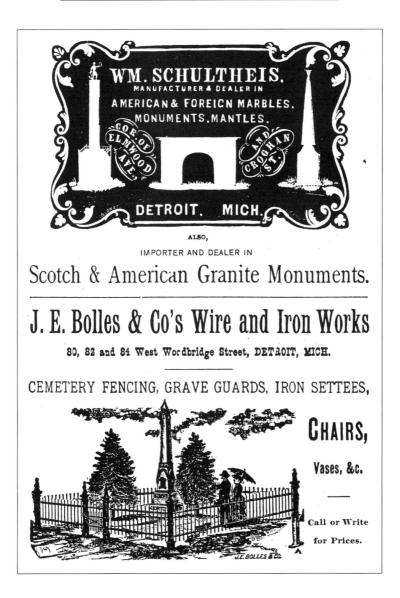

The classic symbol of funerary art—the cross—was used starting in the twelfth century. In Elmwood, one finds many kinds of crosses: Latin, Greek, Eastern Orthodox, Maltese, and Celtic. All of these monument types are characteristic of mid-nineteenth-century funerary art.

Several monuments in Elmwood are hollow and made of gray pot metal manufactured by the Detroit Tile and Cornice Company from the 1880s until 1900. Dr. Levi Rose's monument in Section A, complete with a relief portrait bust, is an excellent example of the skilled craftsmanship achieved in metal.

T. H. ROBERTS,

Funeral Director and Embalmer

31 ADAMS AVE., EAST,

Opposite East Grand Circus Park.   Telephone No. 268.

PROMPT ATTENTION GIVEN TO ALL ORDERS

AT ALL HOURS OF DAY AND NIGHT.

CHARLES WARNCKE,

FLORIST

Wholesale and Retail Grower and Dealer in

GREENHOUSE PLANTS

ALSO A FULL LINE OF

RUSTIC VASES AND IRON CHAIRS FOR SALE.

FORT STREET WEST, NEAR WOODMERE CEMETERY,

Orders for Cut Flowers and Bouquets promptly filled. Special attention paid to the care of Graves and Cemetery Lots.

Being remembered requires not only funerary art but words as well. After passing through the gatehouse, a visitor might find his or her stride interrupted at the sight of the Joy family's memorial peristyle. Helen Bourne Joy Lee's final words raise a smile. The epitaph on her upright marker proudly proclaims, "Never a Dull Moment!"

Near Helen lies her father, Henry Bourne Joy, Sr., a founder of the Packard Motor Company. His gravestone with skull and crossbones is characteristic of a Colonial American style.

Ascending the hilltop where the superintendent's cottage once stood is a rock covering George Pierrot's resting place. Pierrot hosted a local television travelogue series during the 1960s. The rock came from his cottage in Canada; he would sit upon it for hours while fishing.

Near George and his wife, Helen, is a bronze sarcophagus and white granite monument. The hollow bronze edifice in classical relief rests on three large pallets of granite. Beneath the bronze cover lies a stairway that descends into a subterranean vault. Here the Stephens family rests in complete darkness. The white granite is a memorial to the Emory Ford family. Both the sarcophagus and the monument are sculptural copies, with some variations, of the sarcophagus of the Roman general Cornelius Scipio Barbatus, who died in 289 B.C. The original sarcophagus is in the Vatican Museum and was widely reproduced in nineteenth-century funerary art. The word *sarcophagus* literally translates as "flesh-eating stone." Sarcophagi in the distant past were used for actual interment, but here in Elmwood, as in many other American cemeteries, the form was adopted only as a monument style.

In the Hazel Dell section is a beautiful marble urn that once graced the estate of Norwegian composer Edvard Grieg.

On the northern edge of Chief Pontiac Valley, a thirty-foot monument of a fire chief watches over the "Firemen's Lot." Fire hydrants mark the corners of this fraternal spot where Detroit's fire fighters rest among their comrades. On the base of the monument, dedicated in 1876, are bronze plaques depicting fire-fighting equipment and the Firemen's Hall that once stood on the southeast corner of Jefferson and Randolph. The Firemen's Society commissioner, Benjamin Vernor, purchased the lot for $5,000 in 1855. Vernor (buried in Section A) was a bank director who later helped organize the Soldier's Relief Fund during the Civil War. He is also the brother of James Vernor, Detroit's first registered pharmacist and originator of Vernor's Ginger Ale.

Cornerstones mark the edge of the Lakeview section where Elmwood Chapel, dated 1856, stands. The building's limestone blocks were quarried from Grosse Ile and Kelley's Island in Lake Erie. The chapel's Norman Gothic style is the work of Albert and Octavius Jordan, the architects who designed Mariners Church and Fort Street Presbyterian Church. Interior beams that line the chapel's ceiling are made from Michigan cherry and were once held together by wooden pegs.

Limestone also was used to build Elmwood's Victorian Gothic-style entrance gatehouse. The building cost $5,900 in 1870 and was designed by architect Gordon Lloyd (buried in Section Q). Inside the gatehouse, behind the blind arch, is the cemetery's vault, which resembles a huge safe. Here lie the priceless records, a wealth of information for historians and genealogists interested in Detroit and Michigan history.

Twenty-six private family mausoleums dot the landscape of the cemetery, many built into the hillside of Chief Pontiac Valley. These period pieces display craftsmanship from the late 1880s. They were designed by local individuals or firms that specialized in funerary architecture. Considerable wealth is suggested in their Classical Revival styles of Corinthian, Doric, Ionic, and Gothic construction.

The old public mausoleum near the stream's edge is the largest in Elmwood and was built by N. C. Hinsdale's Sons Granite Company of Indianapolis. Inside, the Vermont granite structure contains 190 burial spaces with Italian marble tablets, 96 cremation niches, bronze entrance gates, a tiled mosaic floor, air vents, and skylight windows. The Greek temple in Doric style took five years to build and was completed in 1900. This was the last mausoleum built in Elmwood in the nineteenth century.

Sadly, many of these entombment sites are in disrepair and completely deserted. This is the fault not so much of the cemetery today but of the age of some of its tombs, the materials used in their construction, and weather. In addition, many of the families have died out of Detroit society, leaving no trace of descendants. Close to the pond's outlet, the Bailey mausoleum began to deteriorate the day the sandstone structure was completed. Now, a century later, its marble facade balances on crumbled cement. Entrance to the tomb is denied by rusted hinges that long to grasp a careworn door. What was once a family shrine now resembles the opening of an abandoned mine. One can imagine the beauty of this sanctuary only by comparing its appearance today with a photo taken in 1889 (photos 6, 7, 8).

In 1895, Frederick Law Olmstead, the noted landscape architect who had designed parks, college campuses, and cemeteries throughout the country, came to Detroit and visited Elmwood. Olmstead had gained considerable recognition before the Civil War, when he laid out New York's Central Park. He also conceived the idea of a central driveway on Belle Isle in 1879.

Olmstead was a leading spokesman for a growing number of land-scape architects in the United States who felt that many rural ceme-teries were becoming crowded and cluttered. He believed that lauda-tory monuments added little but confusion to a cemetery's intended naturalism. Other critics charged that rural cemeteries had become nothing more than outdoor exhibits displaying wealth, success, and sta-tus in the community.

An emphasis on simplicity would precipitate the trend of scaled-down monuments in Elmwood and elsewhere by the beginning of the twentieth century. Ideas about burial landscapes led to the "lawn park" or "memorial park" cemetery movement in which monuments became similar in shape and style, less artistic, and smaller than those of the past generation. Examples of this newer style in the Detroit area include St. Hedwig Cemetery in Dearborn Heights, Cadillac Memorial Gardens in Clinton Township, and White Chapel Memorial Cemetery in Troy. Carrying the trend even farther, most burial markers since the 1940s are the flush, lawn-type, one-by-two-foot bronze, granite, or marble memorials bearing only the person's name and dates.

At the south end of Elmwood (Sections 10 and 11) can be found twentieth-century mortuary art in contrasting styles. The maze of funerary architecture seems somewhat eccentric in the old cemetery as seen against the sleek Renaissance Center in the not-too-distant back-ground.

In these sections, only a few monuments are considered unique. The last stone-carved female statue, a throwback to an earlier era, marks the 1925 grave of Millie Booth, a financial patron of the arts.

The Caulkins family monument, also dating to the 1920s, is a curving wall that is original and distinct in design. Henry J. Caulkins was the cofounder of Pewabic Pottery, which still resides nearby on Jefferson Avenue. Accented with blue and green tiles and a mourning vase, it is the only monument in Elmwood that uses Pewabic Pottery. Close by, bronze letters inscribe the name Bloedon-Burns on a six-foot family memorial bench made of pink-polished granite. Near the bench is a large upright marker with bronze effigies on the Rolshoven-Bolton lot. Painter Julius Rolshoven had the marker placed in Elmwood in memory of his family. One of Rolshoven's many well-known paintings is the reclining nude, painted in 1896, that now hangs in the Tap Room of the Detroit Athletic Club.

In the Lakeview section, a memorial bench in Doric style was recently placed on the Tuck lot. The gray granite bench was left in loving memory of James Tuck by his family. "It's the laughter we will remember" are the words inscribed on the bench seat of the monument. A closer look reveals a small engraved circle simply stating that the Detroit attorney was killed on Northwest Flight 255 at Metro Airport on August 17, 1987.

Alvan Macauley, the general manager, president, and chairman of the board at Packard Motor Company from 1910 to 1948, also left his legacy in stone in the Lakeview section. His monument was designed by Detroit sculptor Marshall Fredericks, and it draws its inspiration from Macauley's love of wild fowl, showing two bronze geese in flight with a blue pearl granite base below.

The strangest stone in Elmwood is the angel passing from earth on the Waterman lot. Better known as the Veiled Lady, the bas-relief is carved on a twelve-foot Carrara marble panel. The sculptor, Randolph Rogers, grew up in Ann Arbor and became world-famous, with a studio in Rome. He designed the bronze doors of the Capitol in Washington, D.C., and the Soldiers and Sailors Monument in Detroit's Cadillac Square.

Joshua Waterman had the $10,000 monument shipped from Rome in 1876 as a memorial to his departed wife. On the way to Detroit, the ship carrying the monument sank near the coast of Spain. For two years, the Veiled Lady lay beneath the sea before being salvaged. But more perils followed. On the Hudson River, the monument slid off its barge, only to be dredged up again. In 1919, a violent windstorm toppled the monument, causing the soft marble to break. Traces of the cement patch job still can be seen, and weather and time have robbed the metaphorical figure of some of her former beauty.

The Landscape

Back in the early 18th century, the stream that meanders through Elmwood Cemetery was known as Parent's Creek. Joseph Parent was a Detroit gunsmith whose name appeared as early as 1707 in the records of St. Anne's Church.

A half century later, the stream became the site of a violent massacre during the French and Indian Wars, as described by Silas Farmer in *The History of Detroit and Michigan* and by George B. Catlin in "The Story of Detroit." The siege of Detroit during the summer of 1763 was a series of skirmishes between an Ottawa chieftain named Pontiac and British Major Henry Gladwin, the commander at Fort Pontchartrain. On the morning of July 30, a sortie (260 troops from a detachment of the 60th Foot) was led by Captain James Dalzell to attack Pontiac's camp near Parent's Creek. Dalzell's troops were taken by complete surprise at a log bridge that crossed over the creek. In a few brief moments, about 160 men were killed by a torrent of arrows and bullets. So many bodies fell into Parent's Creek that its waters turned red, and the creek acquired a name that is timeless: Bloody Run.

What is left of Parent's Creek is the gentle water that flows under Jefferson Avenue from the cemetery's large pond. Little did Joseph Parent know that his ribbon farm would become part of Detroit's history, a silent witness to Dalzell's disaster and Pontiac's brief victory, and that his name would be remembered three centuries later.

Elmwood Cemetery encompasses the most attractive natural landscape within the limits of Detroit. It has been referred to as God's Acre because of its carefully landscaped hills, the pond, the stream, and graceful drives and meanders.

Morbid reminders of quagmired graveyard plots in the old city cemeteries were replaced by a quiet countryside that expressed the essence of the word *cemetery*, from the Greek *köimeterion*, meaning "sleeping place."

It was a tradition for Detroit families to purchase entire lots. These formed gardens of graves, not just single gravesites. Many family plots were enclosed with curbstones and steps bearing the family's name, or ornamental metalwork fences full of adornments typical of the Victorian age. All of the wrought-iron fences either have rusted away or were taken for wartime salvage drives.

One of Elmwood's historical treasures is the last remaining cast-iron hitching post, located on the Stenchfield lot. For several decades until the early 1900s, lot owners who lived on nearby Jefferson Avenue came to Elmwood on weekend afternoons by horse and buggy. A horse tethered to its hitching post stood at rest as family members tended to a loved one's burial plot. Grass was cut with a hand-held, whetted sickle. Not only was the stream a part of the picturesque landscape, but water was carried from it to maintain family-manicured flower and shrub arrangements. This pastoral landscape became an ideal spot for social gatherings that would end with a light meal and a jug of barley water.

The scenic atmosphere brought the visitor away from the city and the toils of daily life. The natural environment inspired relaxation and meditation on the joy of life, the reality of death, and the divine. The many artists buried here must have found inspiration in the cemetery's tranquil surroundings while they were still alive.

Nature was welcomed in Elmwood but on limited terms. The landscape is not really natural but instead a product of careful design. Graceful bends and sharp turns in the road were meant to slow the horse and carriage, encourage contemplation, and provide an artistic compositional view of a family monument. Trees and shrubbery were planted in careful order to frame mausoleums and memorials and to balance the pleasing views. Different species of flowering trees, such as dogwood, cherry, quince, magnolia, and azalea, continue to blossom and stimulate a visual response that changes with the seasons—Elmwood's reminder that death is a natural process. Deciduous trees signify the resurrection of Christ. Large oaks embody a steadfast faith. Thorns from the acacia tree represent Christ's crown. Elijah, in 1 Kings 14, wanted to lie down and die under a juniper tree. Certain varieties of forest cover—oak, sprays of ivy, cedar, pine, and willow trees—have symbolic meaning as well. Weeping species planted near the pond's edge in the last century refer to the Greek god Apollo, whose mortal friend Cyparissus died and was transformed into a cypress tree.

More than sixteen hundred trees and shrubs, representing seventy species, are planted in Elmwood. A massive honey locust that stands near the gatehouse is probably the oldest tree in the cemetery. The eighty-foot tree boasts a girth of fifteen and a half feet and dates back to the French and Indian Wars.

As Time Goes By

Hearses first appeared in Detroit about 1830. Before the horse-driven hearse, coffins were carried to the grave upon bars or biers that rested on the pallbearers' shoulders or were carried by hand. Bearers at wealthy funerals were provided with long white linen scarves, tied with linen cambric and used as the bosom of the shirt during the funeral procession.

Alexander Blain was the first superintendent in Elmwood to witness the horseless funeral carriage, a transition that took place just before World War I. But traditions die hard, and during the 1920s, a few Detroit undertakers retained their horsedrawn hearses even after motorized versions became available. A runaway team making off with a loved one could be a ghastly sight, but a number of families preferred the tried and true.

Older folks can recall the days when hand-cranked autos first made their way through Detroit's brick-lined streets. A few of the visitors who were fortunate enough to own this new form of transportation would stop in Elmwood for a short while. Often, a driver would leave the engine at idle rather than engage in the arm-wrenching chore of restarting. Those early-model autos had less than precision gearing or brakes. A car would wander off while the driver was attending a loved one's plot. Drivers were sometimes seen chasing cars down a hillside or uneven pathway. A few monuments were known to have toppled over.

Restrictions soon followed. When the horseless carriage first trekked across Elmwood's gravel roads, drivers had to stop their cars when a horse was frightened. Machines could not drip or smoke oil, and a driver could not honk at a horse or pass a horse-driven carriage or funeral procession.

Visitors to Elmwood are often curious about grave robbing. This was quite common in the mid-1800s. After dark, for example, the recently deceased were exhumed for use as medical cadavers. Cemetery documents do not record any such robberies in Elmwood, even though such crimes were known to have taken place in other Detroit cemeteries. The superintendent's house, which stood on the entrance hill from 1846 till the mid-1930s, was a deterrent to intruders.

Cemeteries like Elmwood, if not patrolled at night, are extremely vulnerable to vandalism. By full moon, the Victorian entrance looks imposing, perhaps inviting some high-spirited fun. Unfortunately, the setting is all too perfect. Once inside, it's not difficult to imagine an ossuary where ghosts walk among the shadows. But often, adventure and prying lead to some form of destruction.

Close to midnight on November 17, 1976, the superintendent, Robert Lupfer, was notified that Elmwood's 121-year-old chapel was in flames. By the following morning, the still-smoking chapel was completely gutted. A group of vandals had scaled the six-foot iron fence, deliberately toppled 150 monuments, and desecrated Elmwood's silent sentinels, statues that had stood for a century, many mutilated and scarred forever. Before the ruins stopped smoking, the cemetery's board of trustees decided to reconstruct the chapel. The costly restoration, funded by insurance coverage and donations by private individuals, followed the building's original plans and specifications as closely as possible, but improved insulation, roofing, and a sophisticated fire and burglar alarm system were added. At a price of $201,724.87, the rebuilt chapel cost fifty times as much as the original in 1856.

The cast-iron retriever that once posed in faithful obedience on the Tillman family plot is now missing, as are the stone lions that guarded the entrance to the Hazel Dell section.

On the evening of July 19, 1992, intruders once again left their mark. They removed the locks and pried open the wrought-iron gates and granite doors of the Buhl mausoleum. They carefully removed the Tiffany-style stained-glass windows, frames and all. For a century, the day's light had entered the Buhl family's stone sanctuary through a colorful haze of glory. The irreplaceable windows will lie dormant for a while, then end up in an antique shop for some unsuspecting bargain hunter.

Elmwood Today

Elmwood continues to reflect the values, conflicts, and history of the populace as the cemetery approaches its 150th anniversary and as this century comes to a close. For the past twenty years, more than two hundred burials have taken place annually in Elmwood. A growing number of these burials result from the tragedy of young people caught up in the senseless killings, the drugs and violence, that plague the streets of Detroit.

Studying the architecture of death in Elmwood firsthand is like reading a collection of short stories—stories that tell of the human drama in Detroit's past and present. In this sense, Elmwood endures as witness to a time of uncertainty and as witness to the internal conflicts of a troubled and struggling city.

In his scholarly book, *The Last Great Necessity,* David Sloane states that cemeteries as an institution will last forever. This is true. The business of death has never been as big as it is today. But we cannot forget that cemeteries are dynamic, and Elmwood is no exception. Cemeteries are born, they live, and they die. Anyone who has walked through some of the family graveyards in Detroit's suburbs knows this. These once-sacred spots have met their own demise. Overturned tombstones, high grass, broken bottles, and unkept mounds are testimony to society's lost reverence.

Each morning, the gatehouse entrance opens, awaiting the next arrival to join Elmwood's silent city, population now numbering more than 52,000. Most will be buried in the ground, but a few will find interment in the public mausoleum built in 1994 near the shallow banks of Bloody Run. Almost a century had gone by since the construction of the old public mausoleum in 1895 before the cemetery's board of trustees decided to add the modern landmark to Chief Pontiac Valley. A stone footbridge dating back to 1874 crosses over the stream, and a walkway joins the two mausoleums. Marble panels from Portugal line the interior walls in the four galleries with glass skylights. Outside, a courtyard of fifty-two underground crypts faces the stream. Designed by Harley Ellington Pierce Yee Associates, the magnificent architecture contains six hundred burial vaults and one thousand cremation niches that will become a temple of memories for the next century's generations.

The completion of Elmwood's new mausoleum coincides with the residential redevelopment of Elmwood Park and Chene Park Commons apartments. Like Elmwood, the new apartments on the other side of the cemetery's wrought-iron fence signal a rebirth of activity in the area.

On national holidays such as July 4, Memorial Day, and Veterans Day, one hears the sound of marching bands, commanders' calls, and volleys from black-powder rifles. History repeats itself as members of the Sons of Union Veterans of the Civil War and the Black Historical Sites Committee pay homage to the Civil War dead who made the ultimate sacrifice for their country. Each regiment stands in formation as the bugle echoes against the cemetery's forest of stone. Taps stirs the souls of all within hearing distance.

A decade of historic awareness has enriched the bus and walking tours conducted on a regular basis in Elmwood. Staff managers Chancey Miller and Joseph Malburg have guided schoolchildren, high school and college students, teachers, civic organizations, historic committees, and fraternal clubs along the tree-shaded roads. Familiar sights on these tours are the blue heron that patrols the pond's edge and the mallard ducks that tend their newly hatched broods. Elmwood is a natural sanctuary of quiet beauty for birds.

Maybe these tours will continue hundreds of years from now when the cemetery is filled. The monuments will have faded, each developing its own character with the passage of time. Even the modest one-by-two-foot bronze memorials will have dulled to green. The unadorned markers of the slaves and homeless wanderers who repose in Strangers Ground will no doubt be completely covered.

Each epitaph is a whisper spoken between the dead and the living. Every letter leaves a mark for posterity reminding the viewer of the reality of death. Elmwood brings the continuum of life and death home to the thoughtful visitor.

On a recent visit, I was caught by the inscription on the Schulenburg memorial that I had overlooked so many times before. Next to a gravel pathway, the imposing monument has stood for a century. A poignant verse on its polished granite was especially appropriate as raindrops fell and the changing season's plant life was once again awakened from the earth:

> *Leaves of the forest sprout and grow*
> *into Springtime,*
> *They fall in autumn and dissolve*
> *into dust;*
> *So come and go all generations of man.*

Once again, the cemetery's tranquil setting inspired the contemplation of death, of the miracles and wonders of life, and the realization that our mortal journey is over all too soon.

Life Stories

CHISELED IN STONE ARE THE NAMES of Michigan's most famous sons and daughters. In Elmwood, the inquisitive wanderer will find more than one hundred last names now borne by the avenues that pass through Detroit.

Witherell, Sibley, Trumbull, Larned, Trowbridge, Brush, Brady, Williams, Cass, Woodbridge, Campau. All are names from Michigan's territorial era, and all are buried along the outskirts of Chief Pontiac Valley in Elmwood Cemetery.

John R. Williams, the nephew of Joseph Campau, was an adjutant general and four times mayor of Detroit. Benjamin Witherell was a judge. Solomon Sibley, whose recumbent ledger balances on an eroded embankment, was the first delegate to the Northwest Territory Assembly.

William Woodbridge, who reposes in Section A, was secretary of the Michigan Territory and state governor in 1840-41. He was an odd character. He avoided bathing for years at a time. Instead, when it rained he would sit contentedly in his front yard, clad only in undergarments. One hundred fifty years later, Woodbridge's favorite rainy-day spot would put him within spitting distance of first base at Tiger Stadium (Broughton, "Spirits of Detroit").

Two steps over from Woodbridge's monument is the grave of his father-in-law, John Trumbull. The revolutionary poet graduated from Yale College in 1763, when he was thirteen, and later became judge of the Connecticut Supreme Court of Errors. Trumbull was also the author of a 1776 political satire, "McFingal."

A few steps from the Elmwood Chapel in Section B are the monuments of two generals from different eras in Michigan history. Charles Larned served during the War of 1812 and was also the attorney general of the Michigan Territory in 1814. His father, of the same first name, was the aide-de-camp to General George Washington during the American Revolution. Near Larned rests his son-in-law, Alpheus Starkey Williams, the Civil War general who was one of Michigan's most active citizens in the nineteenth century. He was a businessman, a lawyer, publisher and editor of the *Detroit Advertiser,* a civil servant, a politician, and a diplomat. Williams suffered a fatal stroke in 1878 while working at his desk in Congress. An equestrian statue of General Williams watches over Belle Isle, but his grave is in Elmwood.

Lewis Cass, a name familiar to most Detroiters, was the territorial governor of Michigan, 1813–31, an appointment he received from President James Madison. Cass served as secretary of war in President Andrew Jackson's cabinet, 1831–36. From 1837 to 1843, he was the U.S. minister to France. Cass represented Michigan in the U.S. Senate, 1845–47, and was defeated the next year for the presidency by Zachary Taylor. From 1857 to 1860, Cass served in his last political office as secretary of state under President James Buchanan.

In his early years, Cass was an explorer as well as a politician. He was widely acclaimed for establishing good relations with Michigan-area Indians and was called the Great White Father of the Northwest. The last years of Cass's life were spent in his Detroit home, where he wrote and published texts on Indian affairs until his death in 1866.

There was a period of national mourning when Cass died. Federal and state courts adjourned, and many Detroit businesses closed. Cass's body lay in state for two days as the public filed past. On June 20, his funeral service was held at the First Presbyterian Church at State and Farmer. A procession to Elmwood was headed by the 17th Infantry and part of the 4th Artillery, followed by militia companies, civic leaders, and fraternal organizations. At the cemetery, high above the stream, members of the Zion Lodge gave the last Masonic rites for their departed brother. A squad of regulars stepped forward and fired three volleys as the coffin of Michigan's most eminent statesman was lowered into the ground (Catlin, "The Story of Detroit").

Across Chief Pontiac Valley from the memorial of Democrat Lewis Cass is the forty-foot obelisk of his political opponent, Zachariah Chandler, in Section B. Chandler was Michigan's Republican leader during the Civil War. He was strongly opposed to slavery and helped further the work of the Underground Railroad. In 1854, Chandler was one of the organizers of the Republican Party at Jackson, Michigan. Three years later, he succeeded Lewis Cass in the U.S. Senate, serving until 1875.

One cold day, the senator was paid a visit by Lieutenant Ulysses S. Grant of the Detroit Barracks. The future general slipped on a patch of ice on Chandler's sidewalk and vowed to sue, which he did. But the two men reached a meeting of minds: Grant ended up settling his suit for the sum of one dollar, and Chandler ended up as Grant's secretary of interior from 1875 to 1877.

Chandler was reelected to the Senate in 1879 and served until his death nine months later. He died at the Grand Pacific Hotel in Chicago on October 31, 1879. A train carrying his body back to Detroit stopped in Niles, Kalamazoo, Marshall, Jackson, and Ann Arbor. Along the way, thousands of grief-stricken citizens paid their last respects. On November 9, a short message was read aloud as his body was lowered into the ground across from Prospect Avenue in Elmwood: "A nation, as well as the state of Michigan mourns the loss of one of her most brave, patriotic and trust [truest] citizens. Senator Chandler was beloved by his associates and respected by those who disagreed with his political views. The more closely I became connected with him, the more I appreciated his great merits." The note was written by Ulysses S. Grant ("Life of Zachariah Chandler").

Nobility

One of Elmwood's most notorious occupants, Albert Molitor, lies buried beside a towering obelisk in Section A.

Born in Germany, Molitor was the illegitimate son of William I of Württemberg. He came to the United States, served in the Civil War, and settled in Detroit. In 1867, he joined Lieutenant William Rogers, an officer with the U.S. Army Corps of Engineers, on an expedition to survey the coast of Lake Huron. Together, they purchased a section of land in a remote area later known as Rogers City.

Molitor eventually owned and operated several sawmills in Rogers City and promoted the area in German and U.S. newspapers. Along with prosperity, however, came a corrupt government, his little empire. Molitor controlled all interests in Rogers City, both financial and political. From swindling employees at the company food store to issuing bonds without voter approval, he steadily increased his wealth by raising the taxes of his enemies so high that they could not or would not pay him. The former prince was approached by a mob on August 23, 1875, and shot while he was working in his office. Seriously wounded, he was taken to Detroit where he died (Rosentreter, "Presque Isle County").

Nobility again left its mark in Elmwood when Count Cyril Petrovich Tolstoi was buried in Section 1 in 1959. The count was the grandson of the great Russian novelist Leo Tolstoy, author of *War and Peace* and *Anna Karenina.*

Born at the czar's summer palace, the count held a title first granted in the early 1700s by Peter the Great. He was educated at Russia's foremost military academy and later became an officer in the Horse Guards. The count joined the Cossacks during the Russian Revolution to fight the czar.

After the revolution, he married a Seattle heiress in Paris and became the owner of a riding stable. They were divorced in 1927. Two years later, he married Gwendolyn Seyburn, a Grosse Pointe divorcee. The couple came back to Detroit during the Depression, and the count became a stockbroker. Tolstoi led a quiet life, with gardening as his hobby. He died at the age of sixty-six at Ford Hospital in Detroit (Treloar, "If Elmwood Stones Could Speak").

The Distiller and the Brewmasters

The impressive sarcophagus memorial of Hiram Walker stands atop the hill of Section A2. Born in Douglas, Massachusetts, Walker came to Detroit one year after Michigan's statehood and started as a clerk in a grocery store on Atwater Street. Twenty years later, he opened a whiskey distillery across the Detroit River. He bottled whiskey known as Club that became so popular that Kentuckians got Congress to pass a law requiring the country of origin to appear on whiskey labels. Walker changed the brand name to Canadian Club, with bold letters on the label.

Walker lived in Walkerville for a short time, but he never really moved from Detroit. He created a ferry line across the Detroit River for commuting to his office from his mansion on Fort Street, where he lived until his death in 1899 (Treloar, "If Elmwood Stones Could Speak").

Bernard Stroh's impressive but deteriorating brownstone monument stands in Section Q. He came to Detroit quite by accident. Stroh, a third-generation brewmaster, left Germany in 1848. He joined a group of German settlers in Brazil for two years and then came to America. Stroh headed for Chicago from Buffalo by way of the Erie Canal. The steamer docked in Detroit. Stroh stopped for a short sojourn, but he liked what he saw and decided to stay.

With $150 left from his Brazilian venture, Stroh established a small brewery at 57 Catherine Street. Detroiters acquired a taste for his lighter German lager beer. Stroh would personally cart small kegs of beer to his customers by wheelbarrow. Detroiters have enjoyed that same "fire-brewed" recipe for more than a century. Stroh died in 1882 (Treloar, "If Elmwood Stones Could Speak").

Another brewmaster who reposes in Elmwood is August Goebel. His twenty-five-foot obelisk is in the Indian Mound section, which contains some of the most impressive funerary monuments in the cemetery.

Doctors

A handful of doctors from the last century made Elmwood the last call on their rounds. Some of the most interesting include Dr. Ebenezer Hurd, a physician buried in Section C who practiced medicine for forty-odd years but never attended medical school. He learned his trade by observing others.

Dr. Henry Walker, who reposes in Section 1, was a president of the American Medical Association.

Dr. Zina Pitcher (Section G) achieved prominent status in the medical profession when he organized the University of Michigan.

Dr. John Irwin is also buried in Section G. His marker used every inch of space to leave a sermon in stone for patients who paid him late or not at all: "Although he was awake to the monetary injustice of dishonest patients toward the medical profession, he left the bulk of his estate to charity" (Broughton, "Spirits of Detroit").

Buried on the entrance hill is Dr. Alexander Blain, founder of one of the first group medical clinics in the United States. Blain lived with his family in Elmwood's Gothic cottage during his boyhood years. His father was superintendent of the cemetery grounds from 1875 to 1915. His granite monument rests where the cottage once stood.

Inventors

William Austin Burt was an inventor, surveyor, and millwright. He built America's first patented typewriter in 1829. His workshop once stood near the main road that leads into Stony Creek Metropark. Burt also invented the T-square and the solar compass, a medal winner at the 1851 World's Fair. Burt's other accomplishments included the establishment of the northern Michigan-Wisconsin boundary in 1847 and surveying the route for the Soo Canal in 1852. He is buried in Section K (Lochbiler, *Detroit's Coming of Age*).

Other inventors buried at Elmwood include Cameron Waterman (Section 2), who brought the outboard motor to the Great Lakes, and Victor Colliau (Section 8), who invented the Colliau Cupola which improved copper-mining operations. Dan Henry (Section H) invented the flowing ship locks and was the planner of the Detroit-Windsor tunnel. Wealthy industrialist Eber Brock Ward, who is buried in Section A, formed the Kelly Pneumatic Process Company, which produced the nation's first Bessemer processed steel, manufactured at Wyandotte, Michigan (Stevens, "Elmwood Cemetery").

Not all inventors made their mark. Sometimes it took a little business sense, and that's what Barton Peck (Section G) lacked. As a teenager, Peck went to work for the Edison Company, where his father was president. He proved to be very skilled with electrical gadgets.

Henry Ford also worked at Edison during the 1890s. Once, a generator was delivered to the Edison plant on State Street. A crew of electricians who came to install the generator couldn't get it to work. Neither could Ford. Young Peck was called in and got the generator to work in no time at all.

In 1897, Peck was the third person in Detroit to build a horseless carriage. He built it in a small shop at 81 Park Avenue. Only a year earlier, Charles Brady King (Section P) became Detroit's first auto manufacturer. Henry Ford followed a month later. King and Ford developed and marketed their inventions, but Peck did not. Some accounts say the carriage blew up during its first road test.

Peck never capitalized on his abilities. He seemed more interested in pursuing the trivial. One of his inventions electrically punished any dog that left its mark on Detroit trees!

In 1928, Peck's body was brought back to Detroit and Elmwood Cemetery after he drowned at Daytona Beach, Florida. He was sixty years old (Treloar, "If Elmwood Stones Could Speak").

Many of Elmwood's occupants left their hometowns in search of greater opportunities in the Midwest. Some amassed great fortunes, such as George Hammond, who reposes in the Hammond mausoleum in Section L. Hammond came to Detroit from Fitchburg, Massachusetts, in the 1840s. By his late twenties, he owned a meat market and slaughterhouse near Gratiot Avenue and Eastern Market. A stone's throw away from the meat market was a fish shop owned by William Davis. Both men shared the same problem: how to keep their merchandise fresh.

Davis invented a portable icebox for his lake trout and whitefish. Hammond asked Davis to use the same technique for transporting slaughtered beef. Davis became the true inventor of the refrigerated railroad car. He died a short time later, and Hammond bought the rights from Davis's heirs. More than a thousand refrigerated cars shipped chilled beef to eastern markets from Hammond's first packing house. The community that grew around the packing house and slaughterhouse became known as Hammond, Indiana.

Hammond stayed in Detroit and began his plans to build the city's first skyscraper. He died in 1888, but his widow carried forth his dream. In 1890, the Hammond Building was dedicated at Fort and Griswold. People came from across the state just to climb to the top of the ten-story building for a bird's-eye view of the city. The Hammond Building was torn down in 1956 to make room for the National Bank of Detroit. The architect who designed the skyscraper, Harry W. J. Edbrooke, also designed the Hammond family mausoleum (Treloar, "If Elmwood Stones Could Speak").

Detroit's Chemokamun

A scrolled white marble tablet lies almost obscured in Section W. It marks the burial spot of Detroit's largest landowner of the last century, Joseph Campau. Secluded from sight, the tablet is quite modest considering that Campau was one of Michigan's wealthiest and most influential citizens.

Campau's family origin in Detroit traces back to the arrival of brothers Michael and Jacques Campau from Montreal in 1708. Jacques, who was Joseph's grandfather, was an officer and secretary to Antoine de la Mothe Cadillac, who founded Detroit in 1701. Joseph Campau was born in 1769, the year Chief Pontiac was killed. Campau died exactly one hundred years after the Bloody Run battle and is buried a short distance away from where the battle took place.

Campau owned and operated trading posts during the late 1700s and early 1800s on Huron River at Lake Erie, the Clinton River on Lake St. Clair, and in Saginaw. Fluent in French and English, Campau also learned to speak many Indian dialects while traveling the countryside. He was respected by Indians such as Chief Maccounse of Lake St. Clair and Chief Wawanosh of Sarnia. They called him Chemokamun, which loosely translates as "big shot." Campau was known to exchange liquor while trading with the Indians. This put him at odds with Father Gabriel Richard, the parish priest at St. Anne's Church. The questionable Indian trading and Campau's Masonic membership explain why he is buried in Elmwood. His wife and children are buried in nearby Mt. Elliott, the Catholic burial ground.

Campau held many civic offices throughout his life, including township trustee, assessor and appraiser, overseer of the poor, inspector of ladders, barrels, and buckets, and he later became a major stockholder in the Bank of the Michigan and Michigan Central Railroad. He was captain of the First Regiment of the territorial militia in 1806 and was a major in the U.S. Army during the War of 1812. Campau and his nephew, John R. Williams (who is buried in Section A), owned the *Democratic Free Press and Michigan Intelligencer,* the forerunner of today's *Detroit Free Press.*

Almost the entire city attended Campau's funeral in 1863. His burial was conducted by fellow Masons and was the largest funeral held in Detroit up to that time. In 1894, Campau's detailed records helped his heirs trace every parcel of his landholdings, worth an estimated ten million dollars (Voelker, "Joseph Campau").

Explorers

Beneath weathered inscriptions are the names of explorers from long ago. Burt (Section K), Hubbard (Section A2), Cass (Section A), Houghton (Section L), and Higgins (Section N) are names of counties, lakes, and towns on Michigan maps. They remind us that Michigan was once a vast wilderness. Until 1805, Michigan was part of the Northwest Territory, which also included Ohio, Wisconsin, and Iowa. Countless acres of primeval forest lay virtually untouched except by scattered Indian tribes.

Dr. Douglas Houghton, who is buried in Section L, was the state's first geologist and naturalist. He came to Detroit in 1830 at the request of Territorial Governor Lewis Cass as well as John Biddle and Lucius Lyon, territorial delegates to Congress.

In 1831, Houghton joined his friend Henry Rowe Schoolcraft on a federal expedition to discover the source of the Mississippi River. Not only did Houghton report on new plants discovered along the onerous canoe voyage, but he also gave smallpox vaccinations to hundreds of Indians. Houghton's reports regarding the copper regions of Keweenaw played an important role in the economic development of the Upper Peninsula. During his absence in the wilderness in 1841, Houghton received word that he had been elected mayor of Detroit. In 1844, he came very close to being elected governor during another absence in the wilds.

On October 13, 1845, Houghton and four others lost their lives en route from Eagle Harbor to Eagle River in the Keweenaw Peninsula when a sudden storm overturned their boat. Houghton's body was found the following spring on the Lake Superior shoreline and was brought back to Detroit. An outpouring of sorrow was expressed for the "boy geologist of Michigan" (Catlin, "The Story of Detroit"). Also reposing in the Houghton family plot is Jacob, Douglas's brother. Jacob led an expedition that discovered many iron ore deposits in the remote regions of the Upper Peninsula in 1842.

A protégé who followed Douglas Houghton into the wilds was Sylvester Higgins (Section N), who completed Michigan's first mineral survey in 1837. He tracked westward to California in 1848 and became an employee at John Sutter's mill during the gold rush. From there, he moved on to Texas and became a wealthy cattle rancher. The Confederacy beckoned with a call to arms, and he enlisted in the cavalry. As colonel of his regiment, Higgins saw hard-riding action during campaigns in the Southwest. He died of consumption in St. Louis a year after the Civil War ended. His body was brought back to Detroit, the city he thought of as home, and was buried in Elmwood (Lochbiler, *Detroit's Coming of Age*).

In his youth, travel and adventure filled the life of Robert Stuart, whose grave rests near that of Lewis Cass, another explorer, in Section A. Stuart, a 32-year-old fur trader from Scotland, led an overland party of seven men into what became known as the Oregon Trail. They were the first to cross the South Pass of the Rockies during ten months of 1812–13. They survived wild rivers, Indian attacks, and starvation. Stuart built a log cabin, the first in Wyoming, to survive the winter cold.

Stuart came to Michigan in 1817 and was contracted as an agent of the newly organized American Fur Company on Mackinac Island. He operated out of his home, headquarters for the company, until 1834. The house still stands today as a seasonal museum on the island.

Stuart and his family eventually came back to Detroit and took up residence on Jefferson Avenue, but their years in Detroit were filled with sorrow. Dates on their children's markers in Elmwood tell us that they were victims of the cholera epidemics.

In 1841, Stuart was appointed by Governor William Woodbridge to be Michigan's superintendent of Indian affairs, replacing Henry Schoolcraft. Treaties he negotiated with the Indian nations had a profound effect on the state's Chippewa and Ottawa tribes for the rest of the century.

Stuart died of rheumatism in 1848 in Chicago. At the time, he was trustee of a company that was constructing a canal to join Lake

Michigan to the Illinois River. His body was transported by boat from Chicago and remained at the Mackinac Island dock for viewing before coming to Detroit for burial in Elmwood. In July 1965, it took a court order by a Michigan circuit judge to keep Stuart's grave in Elmwood. The Sublette County Historical Society of Wyoming wanted to honor him with a memorial at the foot of the mountains near Pinedale, the county seat. But Stuart's heirs objected. As one stated, "Robert didn't even like Wyoming" (Lochbiler, *Detroit's Coming of Age*; Voelker, "Robert Stuart").

Black Heritage

For decades, the students from nearby Martin Luther King, Jr. Senior High School have entered Elmwood on self-guided walking tours to research Detroit's black heritage.

That heritage includes the hardships set upon blacks trying to escape the Fugitive Slave Acts of 1793, 1831, and 1850, which authorized the return of runaways and provided stiff fines for anyone who aided a fleeing slave.

On March 12, 1859, many of the abolitionists now buried at Elmwood met with Frederick Douglass, ex-slave and internationally recognized orator and writer, and John Brown, fiery abolitionist, in the house of William Webb on Congress Street. They met with several of Detroit's black leaders to discuss methods of antislavery. Among those present were William Lambert, George DeBaptiste, Dr. Joseph Ferguson, Reverend William Monroe, Willis Nelson, John Jackson, and William Webb. All were involved with the Underground Railroad, helped organize the First Michigan Colored Regiment, and battled throughout their lives for civil rights and racial pride.

George DeBaptiste, who reposes in Section C, was forced to leave Indiana because of his antislavery activities. He became a personal valet of General William Henry Harrison, whom he accompanied to the White House as a steward. DeBaptiste came to Detroit in 1846 and conducted several prosperous businesses as a merchant. He used his ships to transport runaways to Canada, listing his cargo as "black wool." He also served as a delegate to the Cleveland National Convention of Colored

Citizens and as an agent for the Freedman's Aid Commission until his death in 1875 (Osterberg, "Two Hundred Fifty Years in America").

William Ferguson (Section 10), son of Dr. Joseph Ferguson and grandson of William Webb, was the first black child admitted to Detroit's public school in 1871, and he would become Michigan's first black legislator in 1893. Successful in printing, real estate, and insurance, Ferguson became a lawyer in 1889. The same year, Ferguson and his friend, baseball player M. F. Walker, stopped by Gies's European Hotel for dinner after a baseball game. The two men were removed from the restaurant when they refused to eat in the "colored" section. Ferguson filed a suit that was defeated in the lower courts. With the help of his step-uncle, David Augustus Straker, Ferguson appealed to the Michigan Supreme Court. In *Ferguson v. Gies* (1890), Ferguson won his case when the Supreme Court decided that separation by race in public places was illegal (Osterberg).

David Straker (Section S) was originally from Barbados. Known as the "black Irish lawyer" because of his speaking manner, Straker was a dean of law at Allen University in South Carolina and also an administrator for the state of Louisiana during reconstruction after the Civil War. Straker would become Michigan's first black judge. He died in Detroit in 1908; Ferguson died in 1910 (Osterberg).

William Lambert (Section G) was a community leader in Michigan for almost fifty years. Born in New Jersey in 1817, he came to Detroit as a young man and became an important Underground Railroad agent who set up an organization called the African Mysteries. Members had an elaborate set of codes and rituals for exposing impostors.

Robert and Benjamin Pelham are both buried in the family plot in Section 10. They helped found the *Detroit Plaindealer*, the first successful black newspaper in Detroit. The paper encouraged support of black businessmen and politicians, developed racial pride, and adopted the designation of *Afro-American* rather than *Negro*. In 1889, Robert helped organize the Afro-American League; he later held the position of census clerk with the federal government (Osterberg).

Through the efforts of Fannie Richards, who reposes in Section N, segregation in Detroit classrooms ended in 1871. Born in Fredericksburg, Virginia, in 1840, Richards would become Detroit's first black schoolteacher.

Richards's parents moved to Toronto in the 1840s so their children could receive an education free from discrimination. Richards attended teachers college in Toronto and later studied in Germany with Professor Wilhelm Froebel, an educational theorist who developed the concept of kindergarten.

Richards came to Detroit in 1863 and began her own private school for blacks. Within a few years, she earned a job in a Detroit school known as Colored No. 2. With the help of her relatives and Governor John Bagley, she organized a protest against school segregation. In 1871, a suit was victorious in the state's supreme court. Richards was transferred to the newly integrated Everett Elementary School, where she established and taught Michigan's first kindergarten class. Richards saved enough money from her many years of teaching to found the Phyllis Wheatley Home for destitute and aged black women in 1897.

Her 1922 funeral was attended by city and state officials of all ranks. With the help of Elmwood's general manager, Chancey Miller, Richards was voted into the Michigan Women's Hall of Fame in 1991 (Treloar, "If Elmwood Stones Could Speak"; Osterberg, "Two Hundred Fifty Years in America").

Another important black leader buried in Elmwood is Elizabeth Denison Forth, who was born into slavery about 1793. Her father, Peter Denison, was the first black person to fight for freedom in the Michigan Territorial Supreme Court, in 1807. The case was presented by Colonel Elijah Brush (Section A), a sympathetic white lawyer, before Chief Justice Augustus B. Woodward, for whom Woodward Avenue is named.

Woodward, who found slavery repulsive, had no choice but to honor a 1794 British treaty with the United States which stated that British (or Canadian) citizens living on American soil could not be deprived of their property. Peter Denison was considered the property of his slave master, William Tucker, a landowner and Indian trader who was a British citizen. When Tucker died in 1805, Denison and his wife were set free, but their children were to stay in bondage to Mrs. Tucker.

In October 1807, a Canadian slave owner petitioned the Michigan Territorial Supreme Court to extradite two of his slaves, Jane and Joseph Quinn, who had fled to Detroit. Woodward ruled in the Quinn case that Canada and the United States had no agreement to return runaway slaves. Hearing of Woodward's ruling, Peter Denison and his family escaped to Canada with the help of Brush. Once in Canada, they became citizens and gained their freedom.

Denison's children returned to Detroit in 1812. Elizabeth eventually took employment with Mayor John Biddle (Section F) at the family's Wyandotte farm. Travels with the Biddle family took her to Europe. In Paris, she visited Notre Dame Cathedral and the ancient churches at Saint-Jacques and Saint-Remy. These experiences confirmed her own religious beliefs. She asked in her will that the money from her estate be used to erect a "Fine chapel for use of the Protestant Episcopal Church of which I am a communicant." In 1867, one year after her death, St. James Episcopal Church on Grosse Ile was completed with two bronze plaques on the front door to commemorate the former slave who could not read or write. In 1988, a small marker was placed on her burial spot in Strangers Ground (Osterberg, "Two Hundred Fifty Years in America"; Walker, "Slave Was City's First Black Leader").

Another recent marker belongs to a soldier from two centuries past who is buried in Section F. James Robinson is one of those unsung heroes rarely mentioned in the history of the American Revolution. Born a Maryland slave in 1753, Robinson was personally decorated with the gold medal of valor by General Lafayette during the battles of Brandywine and Yorktown. Denied freedom after the Revolutionary War, he was then sold in Louisiana. In his late fifties, Robinson served in the War of 1812 at the Battle of New Orleans. He came to Detroit and was a preacher for most of his life. He did not see the freedom of slaves until three years before his death. In 1868, Robinson died in Detroit at the age of 115, making him the oldest person buried in Elmwood. He was also the last surviving black veteran of the Revolutionary War.

During the Depression, Elmwood's pathways would awaken each morning as a lonely figure jogged through the mist. Detroit's own "Brown Bomber," boxer Joe Louis, did his roadwork here in complete solitude. Sixty years later, the warm summer nights in Elmwood come alive with the sounds of joggers putting in that extra mile or skating in cadence. Little do they know that they pass within a stride's length of George Henri Slaton, who reposes on a gentle hillside in Section A2. Slaton was Louis's trainer when the boxer was an amateur fighter. Slaton lived near Elmwood and coached the young Louis during morning workouts. The cenotaph next to George is for his wife, the Honorable Jessie Pharr Slaton, who was a judge on the Common Pleas Court in Detroit. Her marble ledger tells the onlooker that she was killed on Korean Air Lines Flight 007, September 1, 1983, when the jet was shot down by a Soviet missile over the Sea of Japan.

Military History

One can see the flash of a saber or hear the cannon's roar through the faded memorials of wars past. Here, military history marches up to salute the inquisitive stroller. Buried in Elmwood are the soldiers, sailors, doctors, nurses, clergy, and political figures who span more than two centuries of wars from the American Revolution to the Persian Gulf War.

The Civil War involved more Americans than any other war in our history. The angel of death reaped its harvest as hundreds of thousands gave their lives during the four years of battles. More than five hundred who served in the Civil War are buried in Elmwood, both Union and Confederate.

A plot northeast of the chapel in Section S was purchased by the State of Michigan in 1874 and dedicated for use "exclusively as a place of interment of deceased Michigan soldiers and sailors of the War of the Rebellion not otherwise provided a final resting place."

The Civil War dead in Elmwood represent all ranks of noncommissioned and commissioned officers. Included are twenty-eight generals, members of a black regiment, two Native Americans from Harsens Island (Joseph Hagler and Jackonat-Bah-Me-No-Ling) of the Company K Sharpshooters, and members of the famous "Iron Brigade."

A Virginia officer who fought for the Union was Major General Philip St. George Cooke. He was a Mexican War veteran who led his Mormon battalion on a two-thousand-mile mission from Fort Leavenworth in Kansas Territory to Los Angeles in 1846. Along the way, he raised the first American flag flown over Fort Tucson (Lochbiler, *Detroit's Coming of Age*).

Some of Detroit's history books recall the first observance of Memorial Day, formerly known as Decoration Day, on May 29, 1869. But the holiday occurred one year earlier, on three days' notice, just inside Elmwood's main entrance. A speaker stand was set up with several national flags and a mounted stuffed eagle. Little is known about why the celebration was made in such haste. On May 5, a mere three weeks before, orders proclaiming the holiday had been issued by

General John Logan, commander-in-chief of the Grand Army of the Republic.

The main speaker, Theodore Romeyn, who is buried in Section B, was a lawyer who earned a reputation as the city's foremost orator. Romeyn paid gallant tribute to Michigan's Civil War dead and asked the spectators: "Let us all show them we appreciate the importance of the principles involved in the conflict, and the value of the triumph ... and let us strive as brethren ... to secure the substantial results of the objects for which our heroes fought and fell." Tears filled the eyes of veterans and citizens as they mourned the victims of a long and bloody war (Lochbiler). Fort Wayne's military band played "The Old Flag Will Triumph Yet" during the conclusion of the address.

Following the ceremony, roses, white lilies, and evergreens were spread among the graves of 205 officers and men from almost every unit that Michigan fielded, including the 24th Michigan, also known as the Iron Brigade, which had suffered the highest casualties of all Northern regiments at Gettysburg. Of the four-hundred-man fighting force, all but ninety-nine were killed or wounded on the first day of battle. A newspaper reporter who witnessed that Memorial Day observance in 1868 ended his column with this: "While the citizens were surrounding the hallowed spot, the sun broke forth and smiled upon the scene. Until late afternoon the visitors lingered in the sacred precincts, and it was nightfall before the cemetery had resumed its wonted quietude."

Michigan men who marched off to war and lost their lives in battle earned for Elmwood a proud distinction shared by only a small number of national shrines. By act of Congress, the American flag is flown both night and day as a memorial to those patriots.

The passing of Colonel Thornton Fleming Brodhead (Section N) is one of the most memorable stories associated with the Civil War dead in Elmwood. Brodhead was in command of the First Michigan Cavalry when it left Detroit for the Potomac in September 1861. He fought in many raids and battles and had horses shot from under him on two different occasions. Brodhead was mortally wounded while leading his men into a charge at the Second Battle of Bull Run on September 22, 1862. As he lay dying on the battlefield, he wrote a last letter to his brother. His parting thoughts became the inspiration for one of the war's best-loved songs, "The Old Flag Will Triumph Yet": "I am passing now from earth; but send you love from my dying couch. For all your love and kindness you will be rewarded. I have fought manfully, and now die fearlessly. But the old flag will triumph yet. I had hoped to have lived longer, but now die amid the ring and clangor of battle as I would wish."

In 1944, Detroit's naval armory near the Belle Isle Bridge was named after the colonel's grandson, Richard Thornton Brodhead, who had a distinguished career as a Navy officer for more than forty years (Lochbiler).

Other Stories

The services of Margaret Mather Findlayson were intoned in Elmwood Chapel on Easter Sunday in 1898. The newsgirl who had cried headlines on Griswold Street became a leading Shakespearean actress on the American stage during the late 1800s. She portrayed a gallery of women: Juliet, Rosalind, Lady Macbeth, Imogene, Cymbeline. A long illness took the young life of Margaret while she was performing onstage.

Thousands of bereaved fans packed the hill slopes, listening as Jessie Bartlett Davis sang gloriously. The tragedienne's shroud was the pure white gown she wore when playing Juliet. Otis Skinner, dean of actors who served as a pallbearer, made these closing remarks: "She was a chaos of beauty, fancy, ambition, sympathy, generosity, all ill-adjusted and treading each upon the other's heels." Margaret's fresh grave in Section 3 was stampeded after the brief service. Fans grabbed pieces of evergreen and rose petals as souvenirs (Lochbiler).

Like New York, Detroit had its version of Tin Pan Alley from the turn of the century until the Depression. Many of the tunes sung in piano parlors across the country were published by Jerome Remick, a native Detroiter who reposes in Section F. Remick was an accountant for his grandfather's lumber business; he bought into the music publishing firm of Whitney-Warner in 1898. Before long, the firm became the Remick Company, one of the world's largest music publishers. Americans loved a good tune. Remick gave them ballads that became American classics: "In the Shade of the Old Apple Tree"; "Be My Little

Bumble Bee"; "I'm Forever Blowing Bubbles." Remick helped a soldier's patriotic spirit during World War I with tunes like "My Buddy," "Till We Meet Again," and "Smiles."

By the time of his death in 1931, Remick had published an estimated sixty thousand tunes. He was honored nineteen years later when Detroit built the Jerome H. Remick Band Shell on Belle Isle (Treloar, "If Elmwood Stones Could Speak").

Shadowed by a large evergreen bush in Section H lies the well-worn slab of Annanias McMillen. McMillen came from Canada during the War of 1812 and settled at the corner of Bates and Congress streets. On September 10, 1814, he and his son Archie were ambushed by a Chippewa Indian party when searching for a stray cow. Annanias was killed at what is now the corner of Griswold and State streets. Archie was held captive in the Saginaw region for about a year, a leather leash strapped around his neck. He and his descendants later became prominent business and public figures. McMillen's slab marks the resting place of the last Indian massacre victim in the city of Detroit (Treloar).

In Section Q is buried Ricktor "Ace" Gutowsky, an easygoing cop who is remembered by the location of his final resting spot. Gutowsky, along with some friends from the force, used to eat lunch almost daily on the hillside next to the Barclay family monument. Hence, their radio call would summon them to meet at "Barclay Square." One summer day, the hapless Ace got a call to duty from his squad car, which was hit shortly after by a passing bus. The accident was fatal. Gutowsky reposes beneath a flat marker near where he sat for his afternoon sandwich. His buddies thought he'd like that (Broughton, "Spirits of Detroit").

The Tombstone's Curse

On a modest hillside in Section L is the all-but-forgotten slate marker of Nathaniel Hickok. Little is known about Hickok other than the fact that he died three months after the onslaught of Detroit's cholera epidemic in 1832. His body was laid to rest in the old city cemetery where St. Antoine Street is located. Eventually, the lonely grave was covered by cobblestones. But why would workmen cover one grave during the making of a new road when other graves were removed? The story is told by Silas Farmer in *The History of Detroit and Michigan.*

Thirty-one years later, in 1863, a repair crew discovered Hickok's moss-covered tombstone beneath the road's cobblestones. Diggers were ordered to remove the stones with the bones, but no one was eager to do so. Perhaps the barely legible words inscribed on Hickok's marker help answer the riddle:

> *In memory of Nathaniel Hickok, who*
> *died of Cholera October 6, 1832.*
> *Good Friend, for Jesu's sake forbear*
> *To dig the dust enclosed here.*
> *Blest be he that spares these stones,*
> *And curst be he that moves my bones.*

The inscription was borrowed from an epitaph William Shakespeare wrote for himself before he died in 1616. For several days, road construction came to a halt. Finally, with the incentive of extra pay and a bottle of fine spirits, an illiterate digger was induced to remove the grave. As for the fate of the unknowing road worker, we'll never know.

The Cemetery in Photographs

I have wandered along Elmwood's pathways for two years to record the cemetery in all seasons and moods.

Photographs

1. Elmwood gatehouse entrance, built in 1870.

2. Von Der Heide family monument in Indian Mound section.

3. Chest tomb memorials.

4. Weaver family memorial in Section W.

5. Beecher mausoleum in Section B.

6. Bailey mausoleum in 1889, Chief Pontiac Valley.

7. Bailey mausoleum in 1993, Chief Pontiac Valley.

8. Bailey mausoleum at the pond's edge.

9. Roman-style death chair in Section L (Augusta Duffield).

10. Chest tomb in Section B.

11. Joy family peristyle monument on Cypress Mound.

36. Fire Chief monument on the Detroit Firemen's Lot.

37. Base of the Firemen's Lot monument.

38. Bronze statue on the Wooley lot (circa 1938 from Berlin).

39. Family memorials in the Indian Mound section.

40. McKinnon family monument in Section K.

41. Kern family monument in Section A2.

42. T. B. Rayl family mausoleum in Chief Pontiac Valley.

43. *Flying Geese* in Section LV (Alan Macauley), by Marshall Fredericks.

44. Nature at work.

45. Buhl family mausoleum in Section A.

46. Albert Molitor obelisk in Section A.

47. Obelisk row in Section A.

48. Chest tombs on the Elijah Brush lot in Section A.

49. Lewis Cass monument in Section A.

50. Moore family mausoleum in early spring.

51. Moore family mausoleum in summer.

52. Dance family monument near gatehouse entrance.

53. Fallen cross marker in Section B.

54. Postmaster James Abbott family monument in Section L.

55. Edgar L. Lewis peristyle family monument in Section 1.

56. General Hugh Brady monument near obelisk row in Section A.

57. Abandoned bridge in Chief Pontiac Valley.

58. Annanias McMillen tablet in Section H.

59. Sarcophagus-style memorial of Henry Billings Brown, U.S. Supreme Court justice, near entrance of Elmwood Chapel.

60. Loring family monument in Section R.

61. Russell Alger family mausoleum in Section M.

62. Levi Grandy family mausoleum in Chief Pontiac Valley.

63. Ortmann monument in Section A2.

64. Count Cyril Tolstoi ledger in Section 1.

65. Booth monument in Section 10.

66. Joseph Campau memorial in Section W.

67. Metal relief monument with ghost wings.

68. A child's vandalized marker.

69. Veiled Lady monument (in Section F, Waterman lot).

70. Elmwood Chapel, built in 1856.

71. A child's marker in metal relief.

72. Eaton monument in 1889.

73. Eaton monument in 1993.

74. Irvin, Eatherly, and Fisher family mausoleums in Chief Pontiac Valley.

75. Baulet family memorial in Section W.

76. Hammond and McMillan family mausoleums in Chief Pontiac Valley.

77. David Thompson monument group in Section W.

78. Duncan family monument.

79. Caulkins family monument with Pewabic Pottery in Section 11.

80. Crypts inside the old public mausoleum.

81. Old public mausoleum, built in 1895.

82. Angel blackened by the elements.

83. Monuments to generals Charles Larned and Alpheus S. Williams.

84. Halmer Emmons Cupelo monument.

85. Praying angel on child's grave.

86. New public mausoleum, dedicated June 5, 1994.

87. Map of Elmwood Cemetery.

1

2

3

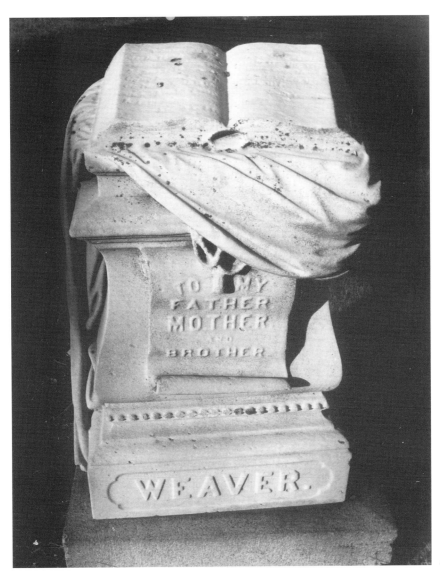

4

5

6

7

8

9

11

12

13

14

15

16

17

18

19

20

21

22

23

24

25

26

28

29

30

31

JACK NA T - BAH - WE - NO - LING
CO. K,
1ST MICH. INF.

32

33

35

36

37

38

39

40

41

42

43

44

45

46

47

48

49

50

51

52

54

55

56

57

59

60

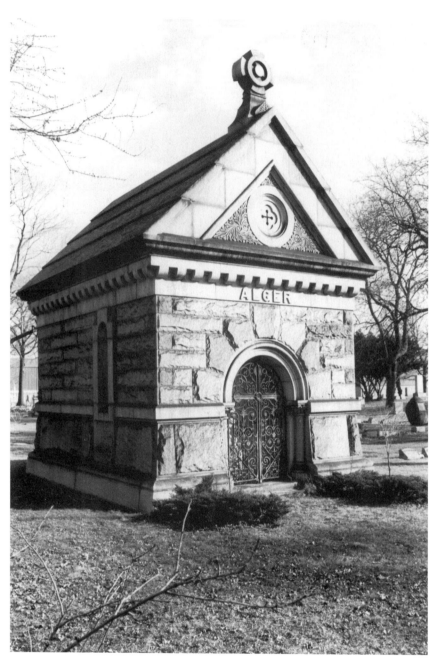

62

63

COUNT CYRIL TOLSTOÏ
1892 — 1959

64

In Memory
of
JOSEPH CAMPAU
Born in Detroit
on the 20, of Feb.1769:
Died on the 23, of
July 1863 in the
95 Year of His Age

His grandfather was a French
officer under the famous Cadillac
the founder of Detroit in 1701.

66

67

68

69

70

71

THEODORE H. EATON

72

73

75

78

80

81

82

84

85

86

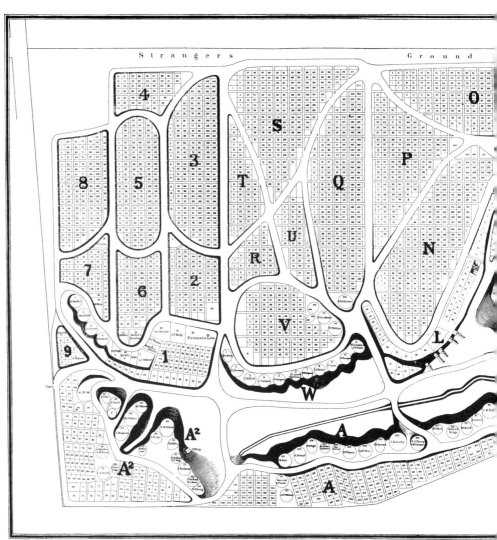

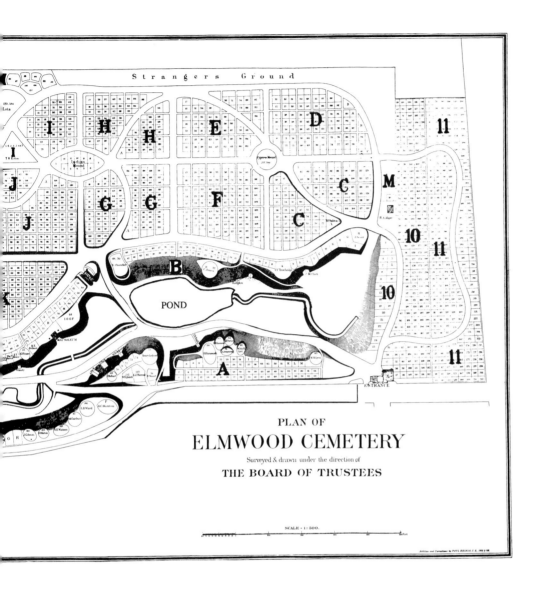

PLAN OF
ELMWOOD CEMETERY
Surveyed & drawn under the direction of
THE BOARD OF TRUSTEES

SCALE - 1:500.

Elmwood Notables in Brief

Governors

Lewis Cass, *born October 9, 1782; died June 16, 1866; territorial governor 1813–31; Section A, Lot 75.*

Lewis Cass was Michigan's most powerful political figure during the nineteenth century, serving the state for more than fifty years. He achieved the rank of brigadier general during the War of 1812. From his associations during the war, Cass received his appointment as territorial governor from President James Madison. He made several treaties with the Indians which resulted in the government acquiring most of the Indian lands within the territory.

In 1831, Cass was appointed secretary of war by President Andrew Jackson. During this time, he was instrumental in Michigan's acceptance into statehood. Cass held the post of U.S. minister to France from 1836–42. On February 5, 1845, he was elected to the U.S. Senate by the Michigan Legislature. He remained in the Senate until 1848, when he ran as the Democratic candidate for the presidency. Cass was defeated by the Whig candidate, Zachary Taylor.

In 1849, Cass was reelected to the U.S. Senate. Well into his seventies, Cass was appointed secretary of state by President James Buchanan in 1857. He resigned after three years when Buchanan failed to send aid to the beleaguered garrisons in the forts of Charleston Harbor in South Carolina before the Civil War.

On April 17, 1861, Cass made one of his last public speeches in support of President Abraham Lincoln's call for three hundred thousand soldiers. Standing shoulder to shoulder with Michigan Republican leader Zachariah Chandler, Cass electrified his audience as he spoke in the Campus Martinus. The mass meeting broke out in a riot, but Michigan raised the troops that were called for.

Cass died in 1866 at the age of eighty-four. He was honored by the state and the nation with a day of mourning.

George B. Porter, *born February 9, 1791; died July 6, 1834; territorial governor 1831–34; Section F, Lot 48.*

George Porter was appointed Michigan's third territorial governor in 1831 by his friend President Andrew Jackson.

Porter was born in Morristown, Pennsylvania, and educated at Litchfield Law School (later Yale Law School). He achieved the rank of major general in the Pennsylvania militia during the War of 1812. After the war, he was elected to the Pennsylvania House of Representatives. Porter served in the government and military of Pennsylvania until 1831.

Porter established the first public school district system in Detroit and the first mail routes in Michigan, and he made treaties with the Indians at Green Bay, Wisconsin.

Porter died of cholera in the Detroit home he was building for his family.

William Woodbridge, *born August 20, 1780; died October 21, 1861; governor 1840–41; Section A, Lot 13.*

William Woodbridge was born in Norwich, Connecticut. As a boy, he moved with his family to Marietta, Ohio, in 1791. He returned to Connecticut to finish his schooling at Litchfield Law School (later Yale Law School). He went back to Ohio and became prosecuting attorney from Washington County and later a state senator.

In 1806, Woodbridge married Juliana Trumbull, the daughter of John Trumbull. Woodbridge's friend Lewis Cass persuaded him to accept the posts of secretary of the Territory of Michigan and collector of customs for the Port of Detroit. The appointments were made in 1814 by President James Madison. Woodbridge was often the acting governor of the Michigan Territory during Cass's absences from office. In 1817, Woodbridge was made a trustee of the newly created

University of Michigan. He was also elected the territorial representative to Congress in 1819.

In 1828, Woodbridge was appointed one of three Territorial Supreme Court judges by President John Quincy Adams. In 1835, he was elected to the Michigan State Senate, where he helped draft Michigan's first constitution.

Woodbridge was elected governor on the Whig platform of "Retrenchment and Reform" in 1839. He served until 1841, when he was elected a U.S. senator. He returned to private life on his Michigan farm (where Tiger Stadium now stands) at the close of his term. He had served in all three branches of government. Born during the American Revolution, Woodbridge lived long enough to see the beginning of the Civil War.

Robert McClelland, *born August 1, 1807; died August 30, 1880; governor 1852–53; Section A2, Lot 49.*

Robert McClelland was elected the ninth governor of the State of Michigan on the Democratic ticket. He was born in Greencastle, Pennsylvania, the son of a prominent physician. He moved to Monroe, Michigan, to practice law after graduating from Dickinson College in 1829.

McClelland was a delegate to the 1835 and 1850 Michigan constitutional conventions. He also served as a member of the board of regents for the University of Michigan. In 1839, he was elected to the Michigan House of Representatives and was voted speaker of the House in 1843. He was reelected in 1845 and served until 1849.

In 1851, McClelland defeated Thownsend Gridley, the Whig candidate, to become Michigan governor. He was reelected in 1852 for a two-year term, defeating Zachariah Chandler, former mayor of Detroit. On March 4, 1853, McClelland resigned as governor to accept appointment as secretary of interior in the cabinet of President Franklin Pierce. He served a four-year term.

McClelland returned to Detroit in 1857 and resumed his law practice. He was considered very conservative. On the eve of the Civil War, he advocated moderation and compromise.

Henry P. Baldwin, *born February 22, 1814; died December 31, 1893; governor 1869–72; Section B, Lot 9.*

Orphaned at the age of twelve, Henry Porter Baldwin went on to become a wealthy businessman and banker. He served two terms as governor and became the fourth Michigan governor to become a U.S. senator.

Baldwin was born in Coventry, Rhode Island. He went into the mercantile business at the age of twenty. In 1835, he married Harriet M. Day, and he moved to Detroit in 1838. In Detroit, Baldwin established a successful shoe manufacturing business and later became a banker. His first wife had died, and Baldwin married Sibyle Lambard in 1866. Baldwin had seven children. Both Mr. and Mrs. Baldwin were active in the community, giving resources and time to charitable and cultural activities.

Baldwin was elected to the State Senate from Wayne County in 1861. In 1868, he was elected governor, and he was reelected in 1870. A devastating fire swept across Michigan during Baldwin's second term as governor. A relief fund of $450,000 was raised for the fire victims. Baldwin's personal contribution was more than a third of this amount. During his term as governor, the capitol building in Lansing was begun.

Baldwin retired to private life upon completion of his second term as governor on January 1, 1873. When U.S. Senator Zachariah Chandler died in 1879, Baldwin was appointed to fill the vacancy. He was unsuccessful in his 1881 bid for election to the Senate seat. Baldwin, who was considered an easygoing and generous man, died on New Year's Eve in 1893.

Russell A. Alger, *born February 27, 1836; died January 24, 1907; governor 1885–86; Section M, Alger Vault.*

Russell Alger was orphaned at a young age but continued his education while supporting a younger brother and sister. He was admitted to the Ohio bar in 1859. The same year, he moved to Grand Rapids and started a lumber business.

Alger enlisted in the Second Michigan Cavalry at the outbreak of the Civil War. He served in more than sixty battles and skirmishes, including the battles of Gettysburg and Booneville. Alger was wounded four times during the war. At the war's end, he was awarded the rank of brigadier general and then major general. He was elected commander-in-chief of the Grand Army of the Republic in 1889. He helped improve pensions for Civil War veterans.

Alger returned to Detroit after the war with his wife, the former Annette Henry of Grand Rapids. The Algers had nine children; six survived to adulthood. He resumed his expanding lumber business as well as interests in banking, manufacturing, and railroads.

Alger played an active role in Republican politics and was elected governor in 1884. He served only one term, then declined the nomination for a second term. Alger was partly responsible for the election of President McKinley. The president appointed him secretary of war. Alger resigned that post in 1899. After the death of U.S. Senator McMillan, Michigan Governor Aaron T. Bliss appointed Alger to fill the term. He was elected to a full term in 1903. He died in Washington, D.C., in 1907.

William A. Howard, *born April 8, 1813; died April 10, 1880; governor 1878–80 (Dakota Territory); Section B, Lot 136.*

William Alanson Howard is a forgotten leader from Michigan's nineteenth-century history. He was born in Hinesburg, Vermont, and was apprenticed as a cabinetmaker at the age of fourteen. Howard came to Michigan in 1840 and worked as a teacher and law clerk while he studied law. He married Jane Birchard in 1841, and they had seven children. In 1842, Howard was admitted to the bar; he practiced law until 1854, when he was nominated for a seat in Congress by the newly formed Republican Party. He was elected in the fall of 1854 and reelected in 1856 and 1858. After his third term in Congress, Howard returned to Detroit and was appointed postmaster of Detroit by his friend Abraham Lincoln in 1861. In 1869, Howard was offered the post of minister to China by President Ulysses S. Grant, but he declined because of health reasons.

Howard became president of the Grand Rapids and Indiana Railroad during the 1870s. He also served on the National Republican Convention Committee and as head of the Michigan delegations of 1868, 1872, and 1876. At the convention of 1876, Howard was instrumental in the nomination of Rutherford B. Hayes. President Hayes appointed Howard governor of the Territory of the Dakotas in 1878. He was inaugurated sixth territorial governor on April 12, 1878. He instituted many reforms that led to statehood for the Dakotas. He died while on a trip to Washington, D.C., in 1880.

Mayors

Solomon S. Sibley, *mayor circa 1806; Section B, Lot 4.*
An attorney who became the first mayor by appointment of the territorial governor. The U.S. Congress gave authorization to plot the new town of Detroit in 1806.

Col. Elijah Brush, *mayor circa 1813; Section A, Lot 73.*
Large landowner, attorney, and farmer. Also a military commander of Detroit who signed the Capitulation of Michigan during the War of 1812.

Gen. John R. Williams, *mayor 1824–25, 1830, 1844–47; Section A, Lot 112.*
Retail merchant and real estate agent who became the first elected mayor of Detroit. The Detroit Common Council was created during his term in 1825.

John Biddle, *mayor 1827–28; Section F, Lot 47.*
President of the Michigan Central Railroad. The Historical Society was organized during his term.

Jonathan Kearsley, *mayor 1829; Section A, Lot 102.*
Military professional and civil servant. Detroit's population reached two thousand during his term.

Dr. Marshall Chapin, *mayor 1831, 1833; Section B, Lot 101.*
Physician and druggist. Daily mail from the East Coast began during his 1831 term.

Levi Cook, *mayor 1832, 1835–36; Section A, Lot 130.*
Banker. The first of Detroit's cholera epidemics broke out during his 1832 term.

Charles C. Trowbridge, *mayor 1834; Section B, Lot 4.*
Banker and railroad man. The city's first real estate tax was voted during his term.

DeGarmo Jones, *mayor 1839; Section B, Lot 21.*
Building contractor and banker. The Michigan Central Railroad was opened to Ann Arbor during his term.

Dr. Zina Pitcher, *mayor 1840–41, 1843; Section G, Lot 10.*
Physician and surgeon who established the University of Michigan Medical School.

Dr. Douglas Houghton, *mayor 1842; Section L, Lot 5.*
Doctor, geologist, and explorer. The Detroit Board of Education was created during his term.

Frederick Buhl, *mayor 1848; Section B, Lot 102.*
Fur trader, merchant, and banker. The first telegraph dispatch from New York was received during his term.

Charles D. Howard, *mayor 1849; Section B, Lot 57.*
Banker and railroad builder. Mariners Church was dedicated during his term.

John Ladue, *mayor 1850; Section L, Lot 28.*
Leather and wool merchant. The Second Presbyterian and First Methodist Episcopal churches were dedicated during his term.

Zachariah Chandler, *mayor 1851; Section B, Lot 49.*
Dry goods merchant. The streets of Detroit were lighted with gas just after his term ended.

John H. Harmon, *mayor 1852–53; Section S, Lot 73.*
Publisher and oil refiner. Detroit's first YMCA was organized during his term.

Oliver M. Hyde, *mayor 1854, 1856–57; Section A, Lot 96.*
Hardware and foundry owner. The Detroit House of Correction and Recorder's Court were established during his term.

Christian H. Buhl, *mayor 1860–61; Section A, Lot 110.*
Industrialist. At the beginning of his term, Detroit had been organizing for the Civil War for three years.

William C. Duncan, *mayor 1862–63; Section I, Lot 8.*
Banker and brewer. Detroit's border with Canada was heavily patrolled during his term, to prevent citizens from avoiding military service.

Kirkland Barker, *mayor 1864–65; Section L, Lot 22.*
Tobacco merchant. Harper Hospital opened during his term.

William W. Wheaton, *mayor 1868–72; Section A, Lot 127.*
Drug and grocery wholesaler. Black children were first admitted to Detroit public schools during his term, in 1871.

Hugh Moffat, *mayor 1872–76; Section L, Lot 7.*
Architect. Alcohol prohibition law was repealed during his term, in 1875.

Alexander Lewis, *mayor 1876–77; Section J, Lot 17.*
Insurance executive and grain merchant. The Detroit Public Library was dedicated during his term.

Ralph Phillips, *mayor 1883; Section A, Lot 192.*
Attorney who helped organize the Goebel brewery. The zoological gardens on Belle Isle were opened during his term.

Stephen B. Grummond, *mayor 1884–86; Section K, Lot 3.*
Marine industrialist. Pensions were established for firemen's widows during his term.

William C. Maybury, *mayor 1896–1905; Section F, Lot 30.*
Attorney and politician. Detroit celebrated its bicentennial during his term, in 1901.

George C. Codd, *mayor 1905–1906; Section A, Lot 136.*
Detroit sheriff 1871–75, postmaster of Detroit 1879. His term saw industrial emphasis in Detroit swing from lumber to the automobile.

John C. Lodge, *mayor 1928–30; Section A2, Lot 9.*
Newspaperman. The Depression began at the end of his term.

U.S. Senators

Lucius Lyon, *senator 1836–40; Section F, Lot 63.*
Judge, civil servant, surveyor general of Michigan 1845–51.

John Norvell, *senator 1836–41; Section B, Lot 135.*
Local politician, judge, delegate at the statehood convention in 1837.

William Woodbridge, *senator 1841–47; Section A, Lot 13.*
Farmer, attorney, local politician.

Lewis Cass, *senator 1845–57; Section A, Lot 75.*
Attorney, politician, Michigan explorer in the early 1800s, territorial governor.

Zachariah Chandler, *senator 1857–75, 1879; Section B, Lot 49.*
Dry goods merchant.

Jacob M. Howard, *senator 1861–71; Section B, Lot 90.*
Judge, attorney general 1855–61, founder of Republican Party in 1854.

Henry P. Baldwin, *senator 1879–81; Section B, Lot 9.*
Attorney, judge, merchant, philanthropist.

Thomas W. Palmer, *senator 1883–89; Palmer vault.*
Lumber baron.

James McMillan, *senator 1889–1902; McMillan vault.*
Shipping magnate, philanthropist. One of the founders of Grace Hospital.

Russell A. Alger, *senator 1902–1907; Alger vault.*
Attorney, lumber baron.

Truman H. Newberry, *senator 1919–22; Section W, Lot 2.*
Politician, philanthropist.

Black Leaders

Cora Brown, *Section A2, Lot 27.*
First black woman in the nation to be elected to a state senate, 1953.

Albert Burgess, *Section N, Lot 149.*
Son of Amos Burgess (see below). First black child to graduate from Detroit High School.

Amos Burgess, *Section N, Lot 149.*
Early civil rights leader (1850s).

Lomax B. Cook, *Section 2, Lot 50.*
Considered the best barber in Detroit during the late 1800s. Known throughout the Midwest as an unbeatable checkers player.

Benjamin DeBaptiste, *Section C, Lot 24.*
Brother of George DeBaptiste (see below). Fought in Company K, 54th Colored Massachusetts Infantry, during the Civil War. This was the regiment immortalized in the movie *Glory.*

George DeBaptiste, *Section C, Lot 24.*
White House steward and close friend of President Harrison. He became a successful merchant and used his ships to transport runaway slaves to Canada.

Dr. Joseph Ferguson, *Section P, Lot 25.*
Physician, community leader, and abolitionist. One of Michigan's first black doctors, he'd been a practicing licensed physician as a "freed man" in Richmond, Virginia, before coming to Detroit.

William Ferguson, *Section 10, Lot 54.*

First black child admitted to Detroit's public schools, 1871. Successful plaintiff in landmark civil rights case before the Michigan Supreme Court, 1890. Michigan's first black legislator, 1893.

Elizabeth Denison Forth, *Strangers Ground, T-45, G-194.*

One of the first black landowners in Detroit and Pontiac. Ex-slave who fled to Canada with the help of Colonel Elijah Brush in 1807. Worked for Detroit Mayor John Biddle's family for more than thirty years. Money from her estate was used to build St. James Episcopal Church on Grosse Ile.

William Lambert, *Section G, Lot 90.*

Community leader for almost fifty years. Important agent for the Underground Railroad and organizer of the African Mysteries. Owned a successful tailoring business.

Robert Millender, Sr., *Section B, Lots 37, 38.*

Attorney and campaign manager for Mayor Coleman Young. Millender Center is named for him. Died in 1978.

Benjamin and Robert Pelham, *Section 10, Lot 54.*

Brothers who helped found the *Detroit Plaindealer* in 1883; it was the first successful black newspaper in Detroit.

Curtis Randolph, *Section 1, Lots 11, 12.*

Detroit's first black fire fighter to die in action, 1977.

Fannie Richards, *Section N, Lot 150.*

First black schoolteacher in the Detroit public school system, 1871. She taught kindergarten and Sunday school and helped found the Phyllis Wheatley Home for destitute and aged black women, 1897.

John D. Richards, *Section N, Lot 150.*

Brother of Fannie Richards (see above). Businessman and supporter of the Underground Railroad. He was instrumental in organizing the 102nd U.S. Colored Infantry during the Civil War.

James Robinson, *Section F, Lot 59.*

Fought in the American Revolution and the War of 1812. He was awarded the gold medal of valor by General Lafayette. The oldest person buried in Elmwood, having died at age 115 in 1868.

George Henri Slaton, *Section A, Lot 48.*

Trained boxer Joe Louis when Louis was an amateur. He lived next to Elmwood.

Judge Jessie Pharr Slaton, *Section A, Lot 48.*

Wife of George Slaton (see above). Judge on Common Pleas Court in Detroit. Killed on Korean Air Lines Flight 007, which was shot down by a Soviet missile September 1, 1983.

Charles Stone, *Section P, Lot 25.*

Orchestra leader in the early 1900s. Stone Family Orchestra played on the Put-in-Bay ferries and later at Fairlane Manor in Dearborn. Henry Ford's favorite musician for social gatherings.

D. Augustus Straker, *Section S, Lot 10.*

Brother-in-law of Fannie and John Richards (see above). Principal of St. Mary's School in Barbados at age seventeen. Attorney in *Ferguson v. Gies,* 1890. Michigan's first back judge.

William Webb, *Section P, Lot 25.*

Attorney, community leader, abolitionist, 1850s and 1860s.

Family of Dr. Charles Wright, *Section 10, Lot 95.*

Founder of the Museum of African-American History. Served on the University of Detroit Board of Trustees, late 1960s, early 1970s.

Lorenzo C. Wright, *Section J, Lot 94.*

Won Olympic gold medal in the 400-meter relay, London, 1948.

Members of the 102nd U.S. Colored Infantry, *Section S, Civil War Soldiers Lot.*

Formed entirely of volunteers from 1863–65, the regiment saw service in South Carolina, Georgia, and Florida. More than fourteen hundred men belonged, and ten percent of them lost their lives in battle. Buried at Elmwood: *William H. Carter, London Floyd, Charles Gilbert, George H. Griggs, Greenbury Hodge, George A. Holmes, Albert J. Ratliff, William Riley, Frank Robinson, Robert K. Russell, William Shorter, Henry Smith, Augustus Stewart, Berry Thomas, Robert Thomas, Daniel B. Walker,* and *Henry Williams.* (Frank Robinson was only ten years old when the Civil War ended in 1865. He served as a drummer in Musician Company E.)

Civil War Generals

More than ninety thousand men from Michigan served in the Civil War; more than four thousand were officers. The highest military ranks awarded were brigadier general and major general. The commissioned and breveted rank of general was held by twenty-eight men who are buried at Elmwood Cemetery.

A brevet rank was often awarded for gallantry or meritorious service under fire. Brevet titles were recognized within the officer's own organization or when he served in court-martials. The brevet title did not give an officer military precedence or pay but was an honorary recognition for extraordinary service. Not all of these men were generals during the Civil War, but all served in that war and were recognized as generals during their lifetimes.

Russell Alger, *Brevet Major General; born February 27, 1836; died January 24, 1907; Alger vault.*

Alger, born in Ohio, was orphaned at the age of twelve. He continued his education while supporting a younger brother and sister. He was admitted to the Ohio bar in 1859 and later moved to Grand Rapids, Michigan, where he established a lumber business.

Alger enlisted at the outbreak of the Civil War in the 2nd Michigan Cavalry. He was appointed captain of Company C. His later commissions included major in the 2nd Michigan Cavalry, lieutenant colonel in the 6th Michigan Cavalry, and colonel in the 5th Michigan Cavalry. He served in more than sixty battles and skirmishes during the war, including the battles of Gettysburg and Booneville, Mississippi.

He was wounded four times during the war and was awarded the rank of brigadier and then major general by the war's end. Alger was elected commander-in-chief of the Grand Army of the Republic and was noted for helping improve pensions for Civil War veterans.

After the war, Alger returned to Detroit with his wife, the former Annette Henry of Grand Rapids. The Algers had nine children; only six survived to adulthood. He resumed his expanding lumber business as well as interests in banking, manufacturing, and railroads.

Alger took an active part in Republican politics and was elected governor of Michigan in 1884. He served only one term, 1885–86, and declined the nomination for a second term. Working behind the scenes, he played an instrumental part in the election of President McKinley, who appointed Alger secretary of war. Alger resigned the post in 1899. After the death of U.S. Senator James McMillan, Michigan Governor Aaron Bliss appointed Alger to fill the term. He was elected to a full term by the Michigan Legislature in 1903. Alger died in Washington, D.C., in 1907.

Thornton Fleming Brodhead, *Brevet Brigadier General; born September 22, 1822; died September 2, 1862; Section N, Lot 107.*

Brodhead was born in South New Market, New Hampshire. He graduated from Harvard Law School in 1845 and later moved to Pontiac, Michigan. In Michigan, he was appointed prosecuting attorney and deputy secretary of state. At age twenty-seven, Brodhead was elected to the Michigan State Senate. He married Archange Macomb, a daughter of General William Macomb. They had six children.

Brodhead was the owner and editor of the *Democratic Free Press*. He also owned the first steam printing press in Michigan and later purchased the *Detroit Commercial Bulletin* in 1851. Brodhead was active in national Democratic politics and in 1853 was appointed postmaster of Detroit by President Franklin Pierce, a position he held until 1857.

Brodhead enlisted in 1847 as first lieutenant and adjutant in the 15th U.S. Infantry during the Mexican War. He was later breveted to captain, then full captain the same year. He was mustered out of service on July 31, 1848, when the troops disbanded.

At the outbreak of the Civil War, Brodhead was commissioned to raise a cavalry regiment. On August 22, 1861, he was made colonel of the 1st Michigan Cavalry. During the course of many raids, skirmishes, and battles, two horses were shot from under Colonel

Brodhead. He was mortally wounded while leading his men into a charge during the Second Battle of Bull Run. His dying moments on the battlefield were spent writing a letter to his brother. That letter would inspire the song "The Old Flag Will Triumph Yet." Brodhead died on September 2, 1862, only two days after being breveted brigadier general of U.S. volunteers.

Henry Laurens Chipman, *Brevet Brigadier General; born February 1, 1823; died October 27, 1910; Section A, Lot 166.*

Chipman was the son of a Michigan Territorial Supreme Court justice. He was born in Vermont, and his family moved to Detroit when he was an infant.

Chipman was captain of the Detroit Light Guard Reserve in 1861. He entered service in the Civil War as captain of the 11th U.S. Infantry on May 14, 1861. He was transferred to the 2nd Michigan Infantry soon after with the rank of lieutenant colonel. Chipman saw battle at Chancellorsville and Gettysburg. He was made colonel of the 102nd Colored Infantry on April 15, 1864. On March 13, 1865, he was breveted brigadier general, and he was mustered out of service that same year on September 30. Following the war, he was made major of the 3rd U.S. Infantry on May 19, 1881. Chipman retired from service on February 1, 1887.

Henry Boynton Clitz, *Brigadier General; born July 4, 1824; disappeared October 31, 1888; Section G, Lot A (memorial).*

Clitz was born in Sackett's Harbor, New York. He attended West Point from 1841 to 1845 and entered service on July 1, 1845, as second lieutenant in the 7th U.S. Infantry. Clitz was transferred to the 3rd U.S. Infantry on September 21, 1846, and was breveted to first lieutenant for gallant service in the Mexican War. He attained the rank of captain on December 6, 1858.

Clitz was a major in the 12th U.S. Infantry at the outbreak of the Civil War. He was breveted lieutenant colonel on June 27, 1862, for meritorious service in the Battle of Gaines's Mill, Virginia, where he was wounded and taken prisoner. He was exchanged during his recovery and was appointed commandant of West Point. Clitz became colonel of the 6th U.S. Infantry and was breveted brigadier general on March 13, 1865. After the war, he rose to the rank of general.

In 1880, he returned to Detroit, his boyhood home, and was made commandant of Fort Wayne. General Clitz retired at the age of sixty-one after forty-four years of service in the Army. He disappeared on October 31, 1888, at Niagara Falls. It is assumed that he drowned, though his body was never recovered. Clitz is remembered with a ceno-taph on the family lot in Elmwood.

Philip St. George Cooke, *Brevet Major General; born June 13, 1809; died March 20, 1895; Section H, Lot 94.*

Cooke was born in Leesburg, Virginia. He attended West Point and graduated in 1827. He married Rachael Wilt in Missouri; they had four children. His daughter Flora married Confederate General Jeb Stuart. His other daughter, Julia, married Union General Jacob Sharpe (who is also buried in Elmwood). John Rogers Cooke, Philip Cooke's son, was a Confederate general.

Cooke was commissioned into the infantry and later transferred to the dragoons. He was lieutenant colonel in command of the Mormon battalion formed in July 1846 to participate in the Mexican War. The battalion's westward march from Council Bluffs to the Pacific covered two thousand miles and was the longest military march ever recorded. The battalion raised the first American flag at Tucson, Arizona, in December 1846; it reached the Old San Diego Mission in January 1847, creating the first wagon train road from Santa Fe to the Pacific.

Cooke was stationed in Utah at the outbreak of the Civil War. He was commissioned brigadier general on November 13, 1861, and was in command of a brigade of cavalry in Washington, D.C. He fought in the battles at Yorktown, Williamsburg, Gaines's Mill, and Glendale. In August 1863, he took command of the troops in the Baton Rouge district. He was breveted major general at the end of the war. He was transferred to Detroit in 1870 and retired from the army in 1873.

Gustaves Adolphus DeRussy, *Brevet Brigadier General; born November 3, 1818; died May 29, 1891; Section G, Lot A.*

DeRussy's father was the superintendent of West Point. He attend-ed West Point himself but was expelled in 1839. He married Frances Clitz, daughter of Captain John Clitz. He entered the U.S. Army in Virginia as second lieutenant of artillery during the Mexican War. He was breveted captain for gallantry at Chapaltepec, Mexico. He served as a regimental quartermaster at Fort Monroe from 1848 to 1857.

DeRussy was a captain in the artillery reserve at the outbreak of the Civil War. He was breveted captain in the artillery for the Army of the Potomac. In June 1862, he became chief of artillery for General Hooker's division and served in the Pennsylvania Campaign. He was breveted colonel of the 4th New York Artillery on March 17, 1863.

DeRussy was breveted brigadier general of volunteers for gallantry at Fair Oaks, Virginia, and for the Battle of Malvern Hill. He later commanded the defenses of Washington, D.C., south of the Potomac. His commission expired on July 4, 1866; he was reappointed and continued in service in the regular army as colonel until his retirement in Detroit in 1882.

Henry Martin Duffield, *Brevet Major General; born May 15, 1842; died July 13, 1912; Section W, Lot 3.*

Duffield was a prominent Detroit attorney and veteran of two wars. He was the son of Reverend George Duffield and Isabella Graham Bethune. He attended the University of Michigan and Williams College. He married Frances Pitt on December 29, 1863, and they had seven sons.

Duffield entered service in the Civil War on September 10, 1861, as a private. He was soon promoted to adjutant in the 9th Michigan Infantry. On March 18, 1862, he was made acting assistant adjutant general of the 23rd Brigade. He was taken prisoner at Murfreesboro, Tennessee, on July 13, 1862. Later that year, he was exchanged and returned to his regiment. He commanded the mounted provost guard for the 14th Army Corps from June to August 1863. He was wounded in action at Chickamauga, Georgia, on September 20, 1863. He was made acting provost marshal general from February to May 1864, and assistant provost marshal general for the Department of the Cumberland from May to October 1864. He was discharged at the end of his service on October 14, 1864.

Duffield returned to Detroit and his law practice. He was an active Republican but did not seek office. In 1898, he volunteered and was commissioned brigadier general. During the Spanish War, he participated in the siege of Santiago. In Cuba, he contracted yellow fever but recovered. In 1903, he was breveted major general.

Duffield died on the fiftieth anniversary of his first battle in the Civil War at Murfreesboro, Tennessee.

Mark Flanigan, *Brevet Brigadier General; born 1825; died October 4, 1886; Section D, Lot 66.*

A native of Ireland and a butcher by trade, Flanigan emigrated to Canada in 1833 and came to Detroit in 1845. He married Sarah P. Saunders in 1847; they had six children. He held Detroit civil offices of alderman for the 6th Ward, sheriff, secretary of the Detroit Fireman's Society, and member and president of the Detroit Board of Education. He also served as U.S. tax collector for Detroit.

Flanigan entered service on July 25, 1862, and joined the 24th Michigan Infantry at its organization. He was made lieutenant colonel of Michigan's Iron Brigade. He lost a leg during the Battle of Gettysburg. He was discharged for disability on November 21, 1863. He was breveted brigadier general for gallant service at Fredericksburg and Gettysburg.

William S. Green, *Brigadier General; born January 11, 1846; died September 21, 1929; Section M, Lot E.*

Green was a prominent Detroit real estate developer, banker, financier, and Mason. He was one of the founders of the Wayne County Savings Bank and the People's Wayne County Bank. He was also director of the Michigan Mutual Insurance Company. He and his wife, Katie, had two daughters.

Green was a native of Boston. He enlisted in the 11th Massachusetts Light Artillery as a private at the age of sixteen. He took part in many engagements with the Army of the Potomac and was among the troops at Appomattox. After the Civil War, he returned to Detroit and was commissioned brigadier general with command of the Michigan militia. He was a charter member and commander of the Detroit Grand Army of the Republic Post 384.

Albert Hartstuff, *Brigadier General; born February 4, 1837; died June 22, 1908; Section W, Lot 6.*

Hartstuff was born in Seneca Falls, New York. He studied medicine at the State University at Castelton, Vermont. He was a hospital surgeon, did postgraduate work in New York, and served under Detroit's Dr. Zina Pitcher at the Marine Hospital.

Hartstuff entered military service as a first lieutenant and assistant surgeon on August 5, 1861. He was breveted captain and later major for meritorious service during the Civil War. He was breveted lieutenant colonel for meritorious service during the yellow fever outbreak in New Orleans in 1866. He was made lieutenant colonel and deputy surgeon general on December 4, 1892, and colonel and assistant surgeon general on April 28, 1900. He retired as brigadier general on April 23, 1901.

During his years of military service, Hartstuff served on the staffs of generals Cook and Rosecrans. He was stationed at West Point, at New Orleans, on the Pacific Coast, and at Fort Wayne. He was attached to the Department of the East and the military department of Missouri. He was also a member of the Loyal Legion of Michigan.

Benjamin Curtis Lockwood, *Brigadier General; born February 28, 1844; died January 22, 1926; Section J, Lot 37.*

Lockwood was born in Frankfort, Kentucky. He entered the Civil War as a private in Company F of the 6th Kentucky Infantry on October 2, 1861. He was appointed second lieutenant in the 54th Kentucky Infantry on September 30, 1864, and saw service in the battles of Shiloh, Cumberland Gap, and Vicksburg.

After the war, Lockwood was appointed second lieutenant in the 31st U.S. Infantry, and on May 15, 1869, he was promoted to first lieutenant. He became a captain in 1889 and a major in 1899, and he was promoted in 1902 to lieutenant colonel of the 17th U.S. Infantry. A year later, he was made a colonel. Lockwood retired as a brigadier general on December 23, 1907. During his years in service, he saw action in the Civil War, the Spanish-American War, and the war in the Philippines.

Cyrus O. Loomis, *Brevet Brigadier General; born April 11, 1818; died September 4, 1872; Section M, Lot 99.*

Loomis enlisted as captain of Battery A, 1st Michigan Light Artillery, on May 28, 1861. He was made colonel of the 1st U.S. Regiment on October 8, 1862. The unit became known as the Loomis Battery. Loomis was breveted brigadier general of U.S. volunteers on June 20, 1865, for gallant and meritorious service during the war.

Henry Rutgers Mizner, *Brevet Brigadier General; born August 1, 1827; died January 4, 1915; Section B, Lot 134.*

Mizner was born in Geneva, New York. He was a direct descendant of a Revolutionary War captain and a governor of New York, and he was a nephew of the founder of Rutgers University. Mizner came to Detroit in 1836 and married Eliza Whiting Howard, the daughter of Colonel Joshua Howard, in 1851; they had three children. He was admitted to the Wayne County bar in 1857.

Mizner was a member of the Brady Guards at the time of the Mexican War. He was a lieutenant and assistant to Colonel Electus Backus at the outbreak of the Civil War. He was made captain of the 18th U.S. Infantry on his enlistment on May 14, 1861. He rose to colonel of the 14th Michigan Infantry on November 11, 1862, and was breveted major in the U.S. Army on December 31, 1862, for gallant and meritorious service in the Battle of Murfreesboro, Tennessee. Mizner was breveted lieutenant colonel on September 1, 1864, for service during the Atlanta Campaign and the Battle of Jonesboro, Georgia. He was breveted brigadier general of U.S. volunteers on March 13, 1865, and was mustered out of volunteer service on July 18, 1865.

Mizner continued in military service after the war and on February 22, 1869, was made major in the 20th U.S. Infantry. He was transferred to the 12th U.S. Infantry on March 14, 1869, and again on May 14, 1877, to the 8th U.S. Infantry. Mizner was made lieutenant colonel of the 10th U.S. Infantry on December 15, 1880. He retired from active service on August 1, 1891. In 1904, he was breveted brigadier general by President Theodore Roosevelt.

Friend Palmer, *Quartermaster General; born May 7, 1820; died October 9, 1906; Section A, Lot 98.*

Palmer was born in Canandaigua, New York. He came to Detroit with his family at an early age and was educated in the public schools and at the University of Michigan. He was in the book-binding business and in real estate. He was also a historian and author. Palmer married Harriet Witherall, and they had three children.

Palmer was appointed assistant quartermaster general for Michigan at the outbreak of the Civil War and held the position until 1866. He then became head of that department until 1871.

James E. Pittman, Jr., *Inspector General and Brigadier; born September 5, 1826; died November 11, 1901; Section A, Lot 93.*

Pittman was born in Tecumseh, Michigan. He attended the University of Michigan and was a merchant and civil servant in Detroit. He was a coal and fuel dealer in the 1850s and a director of the Detroit

Board of Trade, the Detroit YMCA, and the Detroit Savings Bank. Pittman was a Detroit police superintendent and commissioner, as well as inspector for the house of corrections. In 1851, he married Elizabeth Hutchinson of Bristol, Pennsylvania; they had four children.

Pittman's military service began in the 1840s when he served as adjutant of the Brady Guards during the Mexican War. He was a captain of the Detroit Light Guard Reserve and in 1861 was a colonel in charge of Fort Wayne under General A. S. Williams. Pittman commanded the 5th, 6th, and 7th regiments at Fort Wayne and was appointed inspector general of the Michigan militia. He was later commissioned brigadier general on the staff of Governor Austin Blair. Pittman organized, trained, and equipped many of the troops who left Detroit for action in the Civil War, including the Stonewall Brigade.

Andrew Porter, *Brigadier General; born July 10, 1820; died January 3, 1872; Section F, Lot 47.*

Porter was born in Lancaster, Pennsylvania, and was the son of Michigan's third territorial governor, George B. Porter. He came to Michigan with his family in 1831, attended school in Detroit, and later went to West Point. He married Margetta Biddle, daughter of Colonel John Biddle and niece of Nicholas Biddle, treasurer of the Bank of the United States.

Porter was a first lieutenant in the U.S. Mounted Rifles during the Mexican War in 1846. He was made a captain in 1847 for meritorious service during the war. Porter was provost marshal of Washington, D.C., at the outbreak of the Civil War. He was transferred to Alexandria, Virginia, and made colonel of the 16th U.S. Infantry. He was breveted brigadier general of U.S. volunteers in 1864.

John Pulford, *Brevet Brigadier General; born July 4, 1837; died July 11, 1896; Section 3, Lot 144.*

Pulford was born in New York City and moved to Detroit with his parents at the age of thirteen. He attended public schools, read for the law, and was admitted to the bar. He was proprietor of a hotel and foreman of Fire Engine No. 3. He was married twice and the father of five children.

Pulford entered service as a first lieutenant in the 5th Michigan Infantry on June 19, 1861. He was made a captain on May 15, 1862. Wounded in action forty-five days later, Pulford was taken prisoner at

Malvern Hill, Virginia, and confined in Libby Prison. He was exchanged on July 18, 1862, and became a major on December 14, 1862. He was again wounded in action at Chancellorsville, Virginia, on May 3, 1863. He was promoted to lieutenant colonel later that month. He was wounded at Gettysburg and again at the Wilderness on May 5, 1864. He was promoted to colonel on June 10, 1864, and was again wounded on the Boynton Plank Road in Virginia. On March 13, 1865, he was breveted brigadier general by presidential appointment for gallantry in action.

After the war, Pulford was made first lieutenant in the 19th U.S. Infantry on February 23, 1866, and he was transferred to the 37th U.S. Infantry on September 21, 1869. He retired as colonel of the U.S. Army on December 15, 1870.

John Robertson, *Adjutant General; born January 2, 1814; died March 19, 1887; Section N, Lot 19.*

Robertson was born in Portsoy, Banshire, Scotland, and emigrated to Montreal, Canada, in 1833. With no money and no friends, he started on foot to reach the nearest Army recruiting station in the United States. He traveled to Plattsburg, New York, and later worked his passage on a steamer across Lake Champlain to Burlington, Vermont. There, on July 2, 1833, he enlisted as a private soldier.

In the spring of 1834, Robertson was sent to the 5th Regiment U.S. Infantry at Fort Howard, Wisconsin. He served for the next six years as quartermaster sergeant and sergeant-major. Robertson came to Detroit in 1840 after his term of service expired. He was engaged in a mercantile business, Brady & Trowbridge, contracted by the Army.

In March 1861, Robertson was appointed Michigan adjutant general. He was breveted major general of U.S. volunteers on June 27, 1864, for service in the field. Robertson retired from active service on September 1, 1866. He became adjutant general of Michigan volunteers and prepared a history titled *Michigan in the War*. He was a member of the Military Order of the Loyal Legion.

Eugene Robinson, *Brigadier General; born May 25, 1837; died October 28, 1897; Section U, Lot 38.*

Robinson was born in Binghamton, New York. He came to Detroit with his parents and became a surveyor and engineer.

Robinson became a member of the Detroit Light Guard in 1857 and enlisted in the 1st Michigan Infantry as a sergeant at the outbreak of the Civil War. He fought at Bull Run and was promoted to sergeant-major. At the expiration of his enlistment, Robinson returned to Detroit and was made city surveyor. He was elected lieutenant colonel of the Michigan National Guard on October 6, 1881. He was promoted to colonel on July 23, 1885, and to brigadier general on October 1, 1890.

Jacob Sharpe, *Brevet Brigadier General; born July 31, 1834; died April 27, 1892; Section H, Lot 94.*

Sharpe was born in Red Hook, New York. He attended West Point and Dartmouth College, graduating in 1856. He was married to Julia Cooke, the daughter of Union General Philip St. George Cooke (see above). Two of his brothers-in-law were Confederate generals: John Rogers Cooke and Jeb Stuart.

Sharpe began his Civil War service as a first lieutenant in the 20th New York Militia. He was promoted to major in the 56th New York Infantry. He was transferred to the 156th New York Infantry and appointed colonel. He was breveted brigadier general of U.S. volunteers on March 13, 1865, for gallant and meritorious service at the battle of Winchester, Virginia.

Sharpe was a real estate agent and later became a U.S. Customs official. From 1880 to 1889, he was the governor of the northwest branch of the National Home for Disabled Volunteer Soldiers at Milwaukee, Wisconsin. He then returned to Detroit.

David Stuart, *Brigadier General; born March 12, 1816; died September 29, 1868; Section A, Lot 76.*

Stuart was the son of Robert Stuart, a fur trader and partner of John Jacob Astor. He attended Amherst College and graduated in 1838. In 1842, he was admitted to the Michigan bar and was appointed Detroit city attorney. He became Wayne County prosecutor in 1844. As the Democratic candidate, he was elected to Congress from the Michigan First District. At the end of his term in 1855, he retired from politics and moved to Chicago as an attorney for the Illinois Central Railroad.

At the outbreak of the Civil War, Stuart raised two regiments of one thousand men each and equipped them from his own funds. On July 22, 1861, he was elected lieutenant colonel of the 1st Douglas

Regiment. On October 31 of that year, he was elected colonel of the 55th Regiment. He was severely wounded while in command of a brigade in Sherman's division at the Battle of Shiloh. On December 2, 1862, he was appointed brigadier general by President Lincoln. The appointment was not confirmed by Congress, and Stuart resigned his commission. He returned to Detroit and resumed his law practice.

Frederick William Swift, *Brevet Brigadier General; born January 30, 1831; died January 30, 1916; Section H, Lot 23.*

Swift was born in Mansfield, Connecticut. He came to Detroit in 1847 to work in the shoe business. Swift and his brother later formed a drug manufacturing business. He was appointed postmaster of Detroit after the Civil War. He served in that office for eight years. He was twice married and had six children.

Swift entered service on June 17, 1862, as captain in the 17th Michigan Infantry. He was made lieutenant colonel on November 26, 1863. He was taken prisoner at Spottsylvania, Virginia, on May 12, 1864, and was exchanged on August 3. He was made colonel on December 4, 1864, and breveted brigadier general of U.S. volunteers on March 13, 1865. He fought in the battles at Antietam, Fredericksburg, Vicksburg, and Jackson. He was mustered out of service on June 3, 1865.

Swift was given the Congressional Medal of Honor on February 15, 1897, cited for gallantly seizing the colors and rallying the regiment after three color bearers had been shot and the demoralized regiment was in imminent danger of capture at Lenoire Station, Tennessee, November 16, 1863.

William A. Throop, *Brevet Brigadier General; born August 26, 1838; died October 2, 1884; Section H, Lot 73A.*

Throop entered service as a second lieutenant in the 1st Michigan Infantry on May 1, 1861. He was made captain on August 17, 1861, and was wounded in action at Gaines's Mill, Virginia, the following June. He was made major on August 30, 1862, and lieutenant colonel on March 18, 1863. He was wounded in action at Gettysburg in July 1863 and at Cold Harbor, Virginia, in May 1864. He was wounded again at Petersburg, Virginia, on July 30, 1864.

Throop was breveted lieutenant colonel of U.S. volunteers on August 1, 1864, and made a full colonel on December 22, 1864. He was breveted brigadier general on March 13, 1865. He was appointed captain of the 28th U.S. Infantry on July 28, 1866, but declined the commission.

Charles Stuart Tripler, *Brevet Brigadier General; born January 16, 1806; died October 20, 1866; Section B, Lot 31.*

Tripler was born in New York and graduated from medical school at the College of Physicians and Surgeons of New York City in 1838. He entered the army as assistant surgeon in 1838 and was promoted to the full rank of surgeon. He was stationed at various posts in Michigan. In the Mexican War, he was the medical director of the division commanded by General Twiggs.

Tripler was appointed medical director of General Patterson's army in the Shenandoah Valley at the outbreak of the Civil War. Then, upon General McClellan assuming command of the Army of the Potomac, Tripler was made medical director of that army. After the Battles of the Peninsula, he was appointed to duty in Michigan and was breveted colonel for meritorious service. He was appointed chief medical officer of the Department of the Ohio and breveted brigadier general.

After the war, Tripler was posted at various points throughout the West. He and his family resided in Detroit during the last years of his life. He was the surgeon at Fort Wayne and Harper and St. Mary's hospitals. He represented the Army at meetings of the American Medical Association, of which he was vice president. He authored four medical texts for Army surgeons and numerous articles on medical practice.

Luther Stephen Trowbridge, *Brevet Major General; born July 28, 1836; died February 2, 1912; Section B, Lot 43.*

Trowbridge was born in Troy, Michigan. His father was a veteran of both the Revolutionary War and the War of 1812. He was a graduate of Yale, studied law, and was admitted to the bar in 1858. He married Julia M. Buel, and they had six children.

Trowbridge entered service as major in the 5th Michigan Cavalry on September 2, 1862. He was made a lieutenant colonel of the 10th Michigan Cavalry on August 25, 1862, and was promoted to colonel on July 25, 1864. He was breveted brigadier and a major general on June 15, 1865, for meritorious service. He fought in battles in Virginia,

North Carolina, and Tennessee. He was honorably discharged on September 1, 1865.

Trowbridge was made provost marshal of Tennessee after the war. He later returned to Detroit and reestablished his legal career. He was appointed collector of internal revenue for Detroit in 1875 by President Grant. He later became comptroller of Detroit and vice president of Wayne County Bank. He was appointed appraiser of the Port of Detroit in 1903.

Alpheus Starkey Williams, *Brevet Major General; born September 20, 1810; died December 21, 1878; Section B, Lot 94.*

As a businessman, lawyer, publisher, civil servant, politician, and diplomat, Williams was one of Michigan's most active citizens in the nineteenth century. He studied at Yale and traveled extensively before settling in Detroit in 1836. He was admitted to the Michigan bar in 1838. He married a widow, Jane Larned Pierson, a daughter of General Charles Larned, and they had six children. During the 1840s, Williams was active in Whig politics in Detroit. He served as judge of both Probate and Recorder's Court and as alderman for the Fifth Ward. In 1884, he ran unsuccessfully for Detroit mayor. He was publisher and editor of the *Detroit Advertiser* and was president of the Bank of St. Clair. He served as postmaster of Detroit from 1849 to 1853.

Williams's military career began when he joined the Brady Guards in 1836. He saw duty during the Patriotic and Mexican wars. Governor Moses Wisner appointed him to the post of major general in the Michigan militia in 1859. Governor Austin Blair appointed him brigadier general of the 1st Michigan Brigade at the outbreak of the Civil War. He served as a brigade commander, division commander, and corps commander in the Army of the Potomac. His troops saw battle at Cedar Mountain, Antietam, Chancellorsville, Winchester, and Gettysburg. Williams was transferred to the Army of the Cumberland in 1863. He was commander of the 1st Division of the 20th Corps. During the Atlanta Campaign, Williams saw battle at Resaca, New Hope Church, Kolb's Farm, Peach Tree Creek, and Atlanta. In November 1864, he was made commander of the 20th Corps, the first troops to enter Savannah. On January 12, 1865, he was breveted major general. In the Carolina Campaign, he fought in the battles of Averasboro and Bantonville.

After the war, Williams was elected president of the Detroit Soldiers and Sailors Union and was appointed federal commissioner to study war claims in Missouri. He ran for governor of Michigan in 1866 but was defeated by Henry H. Crapo. President Andrew Johnson appointed Williams minister to El Salvador in 1866; he served for three years. He was elected to Congress in 1874 and 1876 but was defeated in 1878. While in Congress, he worked actively in veterans' affairs. He suffered a fatal stroke at the age of sixty-eight while working at his desk in Congress.

Thomas R. Williams, *Brigadier General; born January 10, 1815; died August 16, 1862; Section A2, Lot 46.*

Williams was born in Albany, New York. His father was General John R. Williams, mayor of Detroit (1824) and prominent Michigan military figure. While just a boy, Williams joined the military as private in the Blackhawk War in 1832. He attended West Point 1833–37. Upon graduation, he was made second lieutenant of the 4th U.S. Artillery, and he served in the Florida War as first lieutenant.

Williams served in the Mexican War and was breveted captain on August 20, 1847. He was breveted major on September 13, 1847, for meritorious service. Following the war, he was promoted to full captain and posted to Mackinac Island, Florida, and Utah.

Williams was made a major in the 5th U.S. Artillery on May 14, 1861. He was promoted to brigadier general of U.S. volunteers four months later. He was posted to the command of a brigade on the Potomac and later to Fort Hatteras, North Carolina. He was then assigned to command coordinated forces with Admiral Farragut to capture New Orleans. After the fall of New Orleans, he helped with the naval siege at Vicksburg. Williams was killed in action on August 5, 1862, during the siege of Baton Rouge, Louisiana.

Grover Salmon Wormer, *Brevet Brigadier General; born August 9, 1821; died January 26, 1904; Section K, Lot 87-88.*

Wormer was born near Auburn, New York. He left home at age twelve and briefly settled in Oswego, New York. In 1838, he became a cabin boy on a lake steamer. He married Maria Crolius of New York City in 1844; they had five children. He held several positions before establishing himself in the machinery manufacturing business.

Wormer organized and recruited the Stanton Guard as a captain in May 1862. He was made a lieutenant colonel of the 8th Cavalry on

October 3, 1862. He became colonel of the 30th U.S. Infantry on November 21, 1864. He was breveted brigadier general of U.S. volunteers on March 13, 1865, and was honorably discharged on June 30, 1865. He had fought in the battles at Triplets Bridge, Salt River, Lebanon, and Knoxville, all in Tennessee, and the pursuit of Confederate General John Hunt Morgan across Ohio. Wormer died just before the sixtieth anniversary of his wedding.

Famous, Not So Famous, and Infamous: A Walking Tour

Section A

Henry Barnes, Lot 194. Founder of the *Detroit Tribune.* First colonel of the 102nd Colored Infantry during the Civil War.

Gen. Hugh Brady, Lot 92. Fought in the War of 1812 and the Blackhawk War. Founded the Brady Guards, forerunners of the Detroit Light Guard, in 1832.

Elijah Brush, Lot 74. Treasurer of the Michigan Territory in the early 1800s. Colonel who drew up articles of surrender when Detroit capitulated to the British during the War of 1812. Brush Street is named for him.

James V. Campbell, Lot 2. One of three original justices of the Michigan Supreme Court, serving until his death in 1858.

Dr. W. N. Carpenter, Lot 72. Physician in charge during Detroit's cholera epidemic of 1832.

Henry Chipman, Lot 166. U.S. justice for the Supreme Court of Michigan Territory, 1830–36.

John P. Clark, Lot 167. Shipbuilder and owner of several lake passenger steamers, including the *Wyandotte,* during the 1820s.

Levi Cook, Lot 130A. Treasurer of Michigan Territory, 1830–36.

Robert Forsyth, Lot 59. Agent for John Jacob Astor in the fur trade who lived among the Potawatomi Indians. Accompanied ten Indian chiefs to Washington, D.C., as an interpreter in 1840 to discuss treaties.

Mathew Gooding, Lot 37. Chief engineer of the Detroit Fire Department, 1842.

Daniel Goodwin, Lot 144. U.S. attorney for Michigan under presidents Jackson and Van Buren. Michigan Supreme Court justice, 1843.

John Hulbert, Lot 69. President of the Detroit Board of Education, 1844.

Chauncey Hurlburt, Lot 201. Chief engineer of the Detroit Fire Department, 1837–42.

Cyrus W. Jackson, Lot 94. Detroit coroner, 1850. Member of the Detroit Police Commission, 1852–64.

Philip Lansing, Lot 132. Secret Service agent, 1867. Grandson of Colonel John Lansing for whom Lansing, Michigan, is named.

Henry Ledyard, Lot 75. President and general manager of the Michigan Central Railroad, 1877.

Charles Merrill, Lot 61. Father-in-law and partner of Thomas Palmer in Saginaw Valley's largest lumber operation, 1856–64.

Thomas E. Miller, Lot 91. Publisher of the *Detroit Daily Tribune*, 1849. Vice president of Detroit's first YMCA, 1852.

Albert Molitor, Lot G. Illegitimate son of William I of Württemberg. Helped found Rogers City in northern Michigan, 1871.

Thomas W. Palmer, Palmer vault. First president of the Anti-Cruelty Association, forerunner of the Society for the Prevention of Cruelty to Animals, late 1800s. Owner of the farm that became Palmer Park. Wife, Lizzie Merrill, was the founder of Merrill Palmer Institute, now part of Wayne State University, 1918.

Ralph Phillips, Lot 192. An organizer of the Goebel brewery. President of the Detroit Light Guard during the Civil War.

Lendall Pitts, Lot 146. Internationally known artist who spent many years in Paris.

T. B. Rayl, Rayl vault. Owned and operated a hardware store on Griswold Avenue during the late 1800s and early 1900s, considered the finest of its type in the country.

Alexander H. Redfield, Lot 152. Agent for the Sioux Indian tribes during the 1830s.

Dr. Levi C. Rose, Lot 191. Physician and postmaster of Royal Oak, Michigan, 1831.

Duncan Stewart, Lot 180. First person to ship western wheat directly to Europe. A founder of the Detroit Board of Trade in the late 1800s.

David Stuart, Lot 76. Son of Robert Stuart (see below). General Sherman's brigade commander at the battle of Shiloh during the Civil War.

Robert Stuart, Lot 76. Explorer and partner of John Jacob Astor with the Pacific Fur Company, 1810. Founded the town of Astoria, Oregon. Discovered the South Pass through the Rocky Mountains. Built the first log cabin in Wyoming. Supervisor of Indian agents for Michigan. Treasurer of the State of Michigan, 1840. Mentioned in the writings of Washington Irving.

John Trumbull, Lot 14. Judge of the Supreme Court of Errors in the 1820s. Graduated from Yale College at age thirteen. Revolutionary poet who wrote "McFingal" in 1776. Trumbull Avenue is named for him.

Benjamin Vernor, Lot 106. Brother of James Vernor, the founder of Vernor's Ginger Ale. Fire commissioner responsible for the purchase of Fireman's Lot in Elmwood Cemetery, 1855. Organized the Soldiers Relief Fund in 1862. Vernor Avenue is named for him.

Eber Brock Ward, Lot 86. Introduced the Bessemer steel process to the Michigan area in the 1850s. Michigan's first millionaire.

Charles W. Whipple, Lot 123. Judge on the Michigan Supreme Court, 1839–55. Chief justice, 1848–51.

John R. Williams, Lot 112. Detroit's first elected mayor, 1824. Nephew of Joseph Campau. John R and Williams avenues are named for him.

Benjamin F. H. Witherell, Lot 98. Michigan Supreme Court justice. Witherell Avenue is named after his family.

Buckminster Wight, Lot 108. Owned the first steam-generated sawmill in Detroit, 1837.

Section A2

Edward T. Allen, Lot 106. Accomplished marine engineer who worked closely with Henry Ford on research projects.

J. A. Baughman, King vault. Pastor of the First Methodist Episcopal Church, 1845–47.

Joseph Berry, Lot 32. Cofounder of Berry Brothers Paint and Varnish, 1858.

Charles Bewick, Lot 61. Owner of the first steel-constructed steamer to sail the Great Lakes, S.S. *Braunswig,* 1881.

Charles Ducharme, Lot 52. Founder of Michigan Stove Works, 1871.

Alfred A. Dwight, Lot 89. Lumberman credited with opening the northern part of lower Michigan for commercial timber interests.

Bela Hubbard, Lot 51. Assistant geologist with Dr. Douglas Houghton in the 1830s. Hubbard Lake is named for him.

Ernest Kern, Lot D. Established Detroit's first true department store during the 1850s on the site of what is now Detroit's Kern Block.

John C. Lodge, Lot 9. President of the Detroit Common Council, 1919–27. Detroit mayor, 1928–30. Lodge Freeway is named for him.

Robert McClelland, Lot 49. Ninth Michigan governor. U.S. secretary of interior, 1838–43.

George W. Stark, Lot 8. Dean of Detroit newspaper reporters. Spearheaded drive to build the Detroit Historical Museum, 1951.

Hiram Walker, Lot 45. Established Hiram Walker and Sons distillery, 1858. Financial patron of Children's Hospital.

Section B

Orville C. Allen, Lot M. U.S. consul to Trinidad, 1867.

John S. Bagg, Lot 70. Editor and publisher of the *Detroit Free Press,* 1836–59. Detroit postmaster, 1845–49. U.S. marshall, 1857–60.

Sam Barstow, Lot 89. U.S. district attorney under President Pierce.

Alexander W. Buel, Lot 43. City attorney, 1837. Michigan Speaker of the House, 1859–60. Detroit postmaster, 1860–61.

Jackson Calvin, Lot 65. Accompanied Admiral Perry on his first visit to Japan. Rank of commodore.

Dr. W. Alan Canty, Lot 44B. Murdered Wayne State University psychiatrist who was the subject of the book *Masquerade* in 1985.

Zachariah Chandler, Lot 50. U.S. senator, 1857–75. Secretary of interior under President Grant, 1875. Chandler Park is named for him.

Ebenezer Crosby, Lot 101. Assisted in building Perry's fleet in the War of 1812.

Samuel T. Douglas, Lot 18. Michigan Supreme Court justice, 1852–57.

Rev. Samuel S. Harris, Lot Q. Confederate major on the staff of General Bragg during the Civil War. Episcopal bishop of Michigan, 1879. Great-grandfather of actress Julie Harris.

T. H. Hinchman, Lot 101. Fire commissioner, 1862. State senator, 1876.

Jacob M. Howard, Lot 90. A founder of the Republican Party, 1854. Michigan attorney general, 1854–61. U.S. senator, 1862.

William A. Howard, Lot 137. A founder of the Republican Party. Appointed Detroit postmaster by President Lincoln, 1861–66. Governor of the Dakotas under President Hayes, 1877.

Gen. Charles Larned, Lot 95. Son of Charles Larned, aide-de-camp to General George Washington during the American Revolution. Attorney general of the Michigan Territory, 1814. Father-in-law of General Alpheus S. Williams. Larned Street is named after him.

Robert L. Millender, Sr., Lots 37, 38. Campaign manager for Mayor Coleman Young in the 1970s. Millender Center is named for him.

Jeremiah Moors, Lot 109. Architect and builder who did the masonry work on the State Capitol in Detroit, 1828.

George Morell, Lot 98. Territorial judge and chief justice of the Michigan Supreme Court, 1836–43.

Edwin F. Norvell, Lot 135. Aide-de-camp to General George A. Custer during the Civil War. Five Norvell brothers (buried in Elmwood) fought in the Civil War.

John M. Norvell, Lot 135. Aide-de-camp to General Richardson during the Civil War.

Edward B. Orr, Lot 39. Auditor general of Michigan, 1874.

Traugott Schmidt, Schmidt vault. In the mid-1800s established the largest fur and leather tanning business of early Detroit. His building is the present site of Trappers Alley in Greektown.

Solomon Sibley, Lot 4. First Detroit mayor, circa 1806. Territorial auditor, 1814–17. U.S. attorney, 1815–21. U.S. congressman, 1821–23. Chief justice of the Michigan Supreme Court, 1823–27. Sibley Street was named after him.

Henry Thurber, Lot K. Private secretary to President Cleveland, 1893–97.

James W. Tillman, Lot 97. Established Michigan's first furniture store, 1836. Second father-in-law of General Alpheus S. Williams.

Charles C. Trowbridge, Lot 4. An organizer of Elmwood Cemetery and the Michigan Episcopal Diocese. Explored Lake Superior with Lewis Cass, 1819–20. Indian agent and interpreter.

Section C

Julius Eldred, Lot 64. Owned the richest copper mines in the Upper Peninsula, 1841. Sold a moderate ore sample to the Smithsonian Institution for six thousand dollars, 1845.

Ebenezer Hurd, Lot 69. Skilled Detroit surgeon and county physician, 1819–64. Never attended medical school but learned from observing other doctors.

Elijah J. Roberts, Lot 48. Adjutant general of Michigan, 1842–44.

James Witherell, Lot 53. In command of the Detroit militia at the time of its surrender to Britain in 1812. Territorial judge, 1823–27. Fought in the American Revolution. Witherell Street is named after his family.

Z. W. Wright, Lot 59. Organizer and president of First National Bank of Houghton.

Cypress Mound

James F. Joy. Attorney-scholar who financed and coordinated the building of the Soo Locks. State of Michigan showed its gratitude by giving him 750,000 acres. Syndicate attorney involved in the purchase of Michigan Central, Illinois Central, Chicago, Burlington, and Quincy railroads. Joy Road is named for him.

Henry B. Joy. Son of James Joy (see above). Early developer and general manager of Packard Motor Company.

Helen Newberry Joy. Drove a 1914 electric automobile in Grosse Pointe until the time of her death in 1958. Wife of Henry B. Joy (see above).

Section D

Lyman Baldwin, Lot 82. Detroit sheriff, 1851–53.

Edward M. Cust, Lot 22. Established Oak Lodge, 1837, a French-style villa in Hamburg, Michigan, that became a favorite vacation spot for prominent Detroiters.

Mark Flanigan, Lot 66. Civil War general who lost a leg at Gettysburg. Detroit sheriff, 1861–62. President of Board of Education, 1874. Secretary of Detroit Fireman's Association, 1879.

William P. Fuller, Lot 8. Detroit freelance journalist who specialized in articles on the Civil War.

Rodman Stoddard, Lot 79. Contractor who built Detroit's City Hall, 1850.

Elizabeth S. Whitman, Lot 52. Pioneer Detroit telephone operator, 1881–87.

Section F

W. F. Chittenden, Lot 66. State senator, 1849. Chief port inspector, 1853–60.

Henry A. Mandell, Lot 66. Circuit court judge, 1902–17. President of Detroit Bar Association.

Jerome H. Remick, Lot 28. World's largest publisher of sheet music at the turn of the century. President of Detroit Creamery.

George W. Thayer, Lot 63. Mayor of Grand Rapids, Michigan, during the 1850s.

Samuel Zug, Lot 16. Norwegian-born businessman who emigrated to Detroit, built an island south of the city, and later sold it to industrial interests. Even to this day, however, it is known as Zug Island.

Section G

Joseph Aspinall, Lot 139. President of Detroit Board of Trade, 1864–66.

William Chaffee, Lot 103. Designer of Indian Village Manor, Barlum Hotel, and several Detroit schools.

Barton L. Peck, Lot 36. Third Detroiter to build a horseless carriage, 1897.

Dr. Zina Pitcher, Lot 10. Organized University of Michigan Medical School.

John D. Standish, Lot 45. Owned first sawmill in Arenac County. Founded Standish, Michigan. Descendant of the *Mayflower*'s Miles Standish.

Section H

John Autrobus, Lot 100. Author, portrait painter, designer of a Congressional Medal of Honor.

Martha N. Brainard, Lot 58. Well-known Detroit artist of the late 1800s.

Dan F. Henry, Lot 97. Inventor of the flowing ship locks. Planner of the Detroit-Windsor tunnel in the 1920s. Superintendent of the Detroit Water Works.

Annanias McMillen, Lot 119. Killed by Indians at the site of Detroit's Capitol Square, 1814.

Deodatus C. Whitewood, Lot 44. Owned a stagecoach line between Detroit and Chicago in the 1860s. Constructed the ship harbor at Frankfort, Michigan.

Section I

James W. Farrel, Lot 23. A founder and president of the Detroit YMCA, 1864–65.

Harvey C. Parke, Lot 13. Cofounder of Parke-Davis & Company, 1868.

Indian Mound

Ebenezer Benham, Lot 8. Detroit city marshall, 1848.

August Goebel, Lot 4. Civil War captain. Cofounder of Goebel brewery, 1873. Presiding officer of the Detroit Common Council, 1888–89.

Section J

Alexander Lewis, Lot 17. President of the Board of Trade, police commissioner, and Detroit mayor in 1876.

Rev. William N. Lyster, Lot 118. Founded five Episcopal churches, the first being Rector of Christ in 1846.

Rev. W. A. McCorkle, Lot 117. Assistant pastor to Dr. Duffield at First Presbyterian Church, 1865–71.

William A. McGraw, Lot 1. Banker. President of Detroit Athletic Club. Organizer of the Country Club of Detroit, Detroit Boat Club, Old Club, Yondotega Club, and Huron Mountain Club.

Samuel C. Marquardt, Lot 104. Prominent designer and engineer killed in 1917 when a motorcycle he was testing collided with a train.

Henry N. Walker, Lot 35. Owner of the *Detroit Free Press* during the 1830s. Michigan attorney general, 1843–46.

John E. Warner, Lot 6. Circus owner and operator, 1852–77, specializing in freak and side shows. Mayor of Lansing, Michigan, 1878.

Seth A. Whipple, Lot 128. Marine artist. Several of his paintings are displayed at the Dossin Museum on Belle Isle.

Section K

Henry B. Brown, Lot 102. Associate justice of the U.S. Supreme Court, 1890–1906.

John Burt, Lot 66. Son of William Burt (see below). Surveyor who discovered many mineral deposits.

William A. Burt, Lot 66. Invented solar compass, T-square, equatorial sextant, and typewriter during the early 1800s. Surveyed the Upper Peninsula with Dr. Douglas Houghton in the 1840s. Burt Lake is named for him.

Frank H. Croul, Lot 6. Detroit police commissioner, 1907–13.

John N. Ford, Lot 53. An organizer of the First National Bank, the forerunner of the National Bank of Detroit, in the 1860s.

John W. Keith, Lot 60. City comptroller, 1889. Owner of the Cleveland Steamship Line.

William Keith, Lot 60. Master of the first revenue cutter operating in the upper Great Lakes, during the 1850s.

Alfred Russel, Lot 33. U.S. district attorney who exposed the Knights of the Golden Circle, an organization that planned the overthrow of the government during President Lincoln's term.

Martin A. Swain, Lot 74. Marine salvage expert who was credited with the salvage of 358 vessels valued at twenty-five million dollars at the turn of the century.

Lakeview

Edwin W. Denby, Lot 20. Secretary of the Navy under President Harding. Achieved early fame as a young congressman when he resigned to enlist in the Army in World War I. Denby High School is named for him.

Alvan Macauley, Lot 5. General manager, president, and chairman of Packard Motor Company, 1910–48.

Dr. Burt Shurly, Lot 17. Physician at Harper Hospital. A founder of the Detroit Medical College.

James Tuck, Lot 4. Attorney. A passenger killed in crash of Northwest Flight 255 at Metro Airport on August 17, 1987.

Charles B. Warren, Lot 2. International lawyer and U.S. ambassador to Japan in the early 1900s.

Section L

James A. Abbott, Lot 41. Detroit postmaster and justice of the peace, 1806–31. Uncle of painter James Abbott McNeil Whistler.

William Barclay, Lot 42. Superintendent of the Detroit Water Works, 1840–43. Police superintendent, 1862.

Rev. R. Bury, Lot 2. Rector of St. Paul's Cathedral, 1830–33.

George S. Davis, Lot 39. Cofounder of Parke-Davis & Company, 1868.

Solomon Davis, Lot 39. As superintendent of the Detroit Water Works, laid the original wooden sewer lines, 1830.

Julian S. Dickinson, Lot 48. Officer in charge of the 4th Michigan Cavalry detachment, which captured President Jefferson Davis of the Confederacy on May 10, 1865, at Wilcox Mills near Macon, Georgia.

Elon Farnsworth, Lot 33. First chancellor of the Michigan Circuit Court, 1835–43. Michigan attorney general, 1843–45. An organizer of the Michigan Central Railroad.

George A. Hammond, Hammond vault. Founder of Hammond, Indiana. Meatpacker and developer of the refrigerated railroad car for shipping meat in the 1860s.

Dr. Douglas Houghton, Lot 5. State geologist, explorer, physician. Mayor of Detroit, 1842. Drowned at Eagle Harbor in 1845. Houghton Lake is named for him.

Jacob Houghton, Lot 5. Brother of Douglas Houghton (see above). Discovered many rich iron ore deposits in the Upper Peninsula, 1842. Andrew Carnegie was in the exploration party. Sold Carnegie his first iron mine, 1852.

George Van Ness Lothrop, Lot 29. Michigan attorney general, 1848–51. U.S. minister to Russia under President Cleveland, 1885.

James McMillan, McMillan vault. U.S. senator during the 1880s. An owner of the Detroit and Cleveland Steam Navigation Company.

Section M

Emma S. Berry, Lot H. Assistant treasurer of the Confederacy and an aide to President Jefferson Davis. Her signature appears in some issues of Confederate paper money.

Walter J. Drake, Lot 90. Organizer and president of Hupp Motor Automobile Company, 1908. Assistant secretary of commerce under President Hoover.

Joshua S. Ingalls, Lot F. Largest distributor of kerosene fuel oil in the United States during the 1880s.

Anthony TenEyck, Lot 123. U.S. commissioner to the Sandwich Islands (Hawaii), 1848.

Section N

John Blessed, Lot 12. One of the last stagecoach drivers in Michigan. Drove the Plank Road out Grand River between Detroit and Lansing for sixteen years until 1872.

Thornton F. Brodhead, Lot 107. Detroit postmaster, 1853. Civil War general.

Horace M. Dean, Lot 122. Detroit police commissioner, 1876–91.

James D. Elderskin, Lot 174. As a sergeant and color bearer during the Mexican War, carried the first American flag into Mexican territory on May 8, 1846.

John Farmer, Lot 210. Surveyor, mapmaker, engraver, and publisher of the early history of Detroit from 1826–59.

Silas Farmer, Lot 210. Continued the work of his father, John Farmer (see above), writing and publishing a two-volume history of Detroit and Michigan, 1890.

Sylvester Higgins, Lot 70. Geologist who completed Michigan's first mineral survey, 1837. An employee at Sutter's Mill during the California gold rush. Higgins Lake in northern Michigan is named for him.

Elizabeth R. Johnson, Lot 32. Charter member of the Fine Arts Society. Vice president of the Conservatory of Music, 1888.

Francis Martin, Lot 167. Second mate on the U.S.S. *Fessenden* when it docked at St. Helena Isle in 1821 as Napoleon Bonaparte was dying there. Witnessed Napoleon's burial. Born in 1800 and died in 1901.

Arouet Richmond, Lot 204. A founder of the Richmond-Backus Company, which specialized in bookbinding, in the 1840s.

John Robertson, Lot 19. Adjutant general of the Michigan district, 1861–87.

Patrick Stewart, Lot 118. Built the Stewart automobile (only five were built). Founded Stewart Foundry, which specialized in manhole covers.

Edward R. Viger, Lot 63. Captain of the steamer *Mary Queen*, 1859.

Section O

Richard "Maserati Rick" Carter, Lot 18. Drug dealer killed by his enemies at Mt. Carmel Hospital, 1988. His coffin simulated a luxury Mercedes, with grille, taillights, and Goodyear Eagle radials, at a cost of sixteen thousand dollars.

John A. Francombe, Lot A. Owner of the steamships *W. A. Stafford, John A. Francombe,* and *Edward McWilliams* until 1912.

Porter B. Kibbee, Lot 143. Probate judge of Macomb County, 1853–61.

Alexander McLeod, Lot 98. Second mate and part owner of the freighter *John Owen.* Secretary to Mayor Pingree in the 1890s. Wayne County treasurer.

Adna Merritt, Lot 141. City marshall and constable, 1825–31.

James W. Millen, Lot 24. Served on several ore barges and on the schooner *Flying Cloud*, 1856. Owned the ships *Grey Hound* and *City of Toledo.* President of the Lake Carriers Association in the late 1800s.

John C. Sabine, Lot 148. Credited with naming Belle Isle after Governor Lewis Cass's daughter Isabelle in the 1840s.

Arthur Welton, Lot 10. Publisher and banker who initiated the Federal Reserve System, 1913.

Section P

W. E. Armitage, Lot 143. Bishop of Wisconsin. First rector of St. John's Episcopal Church of Detroit, 1859.

John Blindbury, Lot 17. Opened the Blindbury Hotel, 1852, located at the present site of the Detroit Cadillac Hotel.

E. Caroline Campbell, Lot 53. Taught English for forty-five years at Central High School.

George N. Fletcher, Lot 128. His lumberyard in Alpena in 1887 covered five city blocks. Dressed twenty million board feet a year for sale to East Coast markets.

Robert B. Hopkins, Lot 48. Noted marine artist from the early 1900s.

Charles B. King, Lot 128. Built the first horseless carriage in Detroit, 1896.

Augustus Ruoff, Lot 15. President of Ruoff brewery, 1850–95.

Arthur T. Waterfall, Lot 10. Vice president of Dodge Brothers Automobile Manufacturing Company in the early 1900s.

Section Q

Jessie Chase, Lot 158. Head of the Detroit Library branches for forty-five years until 1920.

Rev. Supply Chase, Lot 158. Pastor of the Second Baptist Church, 1861–64.

Rev. Romauld B. Des Roches, Lot 65. Founder and pastor of the First Baptist Church, 1857.

Cleveland Hunt, Lot 196. A founder of Grace Hospital who underwent one of the first cataract operations, 1895.

Elias W. Jones, Lot 54. Supervisor of the Ann Arbor public schools, 1871.

David McCormick, Lot 114. Keeper of Detroit's city clock, 1871–1934. The clock was second in size only to Big Ben in London.

Martin Scholl, Lot 47. Masonry contractor responsible for building Western and Northwestern high schools in the 1920s.

Bernard Stroh, Lot 9. Founder of Stroh brewery, 1850.

Edward O. Trowbridge, Lot 92. Transportation engineer in Spain, Mexico, and South America, 1890–1913.

Daniel T. Wells, Lot 200. Civil War major. Brother of the founder of Wells Fargo and Company.

Section R

John Mix Stanley, Lot 5. Artist who painted *The Conspiracy of Pontiac.* A founder of the National Gallery of American Art in Washington, D.C., 1861.

Section S

Rollin C. Allen, Lot 119. Made the U.S. geological survey of Colorado, 1905–08. A geologist for the State of Michigan, 1909.

Charles H. Borgman, Lot 60. Detroit city clerk, 1878–82. Wayne County judge, 1882.

James W. Candler, Lot 30. Third officer on the *Shepard,* which sailed for fifty days through the Straits of Magellan in 1853. Owner of several sailing ships including the *Cora,* one of the last slave ships, which sailed in 1864.

Civil War soldiers, Lot 14. The Civil War lot contains the remains of 205 officers and enlisted men who fought in the Civil War. Many belonged to the Iron Brigade, which was nearly wiped out but stopped the Rebel advance by sheer tenacity on the first day of the Battle of Gettysburg.

Edward Felder, Lot 1. Author of the first German-American grammar book published in America, circa 1860.

John H. Harmon, Lot 73. Co-owner of the *Detroit Free Press*, 1842. Port of Detroit customs collector, 1853–57.

Walter Harper and Nancy Martin, Lot 177. Donated land and money to establish Harper Hospital during the Civil War. Harper Avenue was named in his honor. Martin Place was named in her honor.

George Hebden, Lot 112. Detroit prosecuting attorney during the 1860s.

David A. Molitor, Lot 65. Nephew of Albert Molitor. Civil engineer and textbook author. Surveyed and drew up the map of Elmwood Cemetery, 1896. Designed the dams and sluices of the Panama Canal, 1906.

Hester J. Spinning, Lot 76. Society editor of the *Detroit Tribune* during the late 1800s. Charter member of the Detroit Press Club.

George W. Walverton, Lot 91. Sailed out of New Bedford, Massachusetts, on the whaler *Cupola* to the North Pacific and Arctic oceans during the 1830s. Great Lakes shipmaster and marine inspector in Detroit during the 1840s.

Section T

Absolom J. Backus, Lot 37. Supervised construction of an eight-hundred-mile telegraph line from Niagara Falls to the Gulf of St. Lawrence, 1845. Invented a type of wood-burning furnace.

Thomas Berry, Lot 48. A founder of Berry Brothers Paint and Varnish, 1858.

Section U

David George, Lot C. Songwriter whose works included "The Wreck of Old 97," about 1900.

James H. Pound, Sr., Lot 34. British soldier wounded at the Battle of New Orleans during the War of 1812.

August Rasch, Lot 10. Donated the land where Packard Motor built its first manufacturing facilities, about 1910.

Section V

Katherine N. Brevoot, Lot 48. A lineal descendant of Henry IV of France.

Henry B. Bristol, Lot 48. Attended West Point at age fifteen. Conducted an extensive campaign against the Apache Indians as commandant of Fort Reno during the Civil War.

Dr. Henry Cowie, Lot 81. One of Michigan's first practicing dentists, 1862.

Frederick Crebben, Lot 108. Owner of the first summer home built at the St. Clair flats, 1897.

William J. Funke, Lot 77. Commodore of the Detroit Yacht Club, 1903.

John Kendall, Lot 86. Headed the Detroit Fire Department for many years (1870s).

Dr. Peter Klein, Lot 8. At age fifteen in 1828, crossed the Atlantic from France to New York in eighty-eight days aboard a sailing sloop. Prominent Detroit physician, 1846–1900.

William F. Lamson, Lot 31. Superintendent of the Detroit House of Correction during the 1870s.

Edward S. Leadbeater, Lot 115. Detroit city treasurer, 1866–71.

Dr. Henry Lemke, Lot 8. Detroit city physician, 1845–46.

John Mack, Lot 9. Supervisor of Hamtramck, 1849–62. Mack Avenue is named for him.

Section W

Joseph Campau, Lot 4. Large landowner and original trustee of Detroit at its incorporation in 1802. Joseph Campau Street is named after him.

Donald M. Dickinson, Lot 7. U.S. postmaster general, 1887.

Rev. George Duffield, Lot 3. Wrote the hymn "Stand Up, Stand Up for Jesus" in the 1800s.

Truman H. Newberry, Lot 2. Secretary of the Navy under President Theodore Roosevelt, 1901.

Section 1

Rev. Thomas F. Davies, Lot 7. Third Episcopal bishop of Michigan, 1889–1905.

George Hendrie, Lot 10. A cofounder of the Detroit Symphony Orchestra, 1859.

Samuel E. Pittman, Jr., Lot 62. Aide-de-camp to General Alpheus S. Williams, 1862.

Count Cyril Tolstoi, Lot 6. Officer in the Horse Guards of the Imperial Russian Army and grandson of Russian novelist Leo Tolstoy, 1893–1959.

Dr. Henry O. Walker, Lot 61. President of the American Medical Association in the early 1900s.

Ross Wilkins, Lot 7. Michigan's first U.S. district judge, 1836–70.

William D. Wilkins, Lot 7. U.S. circuit judge, 1857–70. Brevet lieutenant colonel at the end of the Civil War.

William Wreford, Lot 4. Rented his house and barn on Bagley Avenue to Henry Ford for sixteen dollars a month. Ford built his first automobile there in 1896.

Section 2

William R. Antisdel, Lot 9. Music and drama critic. Author of *The History of American Drama*, 1916.

Charles H. Brennen, Lot 69. Member of the 1896 U.S. Olympic wrestling team.

Angus McKay, Lot 10. Shipbuilder (1807–73) who was the first to use a propeller-driven schooner, the *George Foote*, on the Great Lakes.

Samuel Thompson, Lot 4K. Hall of Fame baseball player. Played with the Detroits (1881–88), Pittsburgh (1889–98), and the Tigers (1907).

Cameron B. Waterman, Lot 57. Invented the outboard motor, 1905.

Section 3

Margaret M. Findlayson, Lot 134. Leading Shakespearean actress during the late 1800s.

Philip A. Hartswell, Lot 62. Artist known for his oil landscapes, 1867–95.

Christian Traub, Lot 6. Founder of Detroit's top jewelry business during the 1850s.

Section 5

Alexander Mckay, Lot 113. Commodore of the Detroit and Cleveland Steam Navigation Company passenger ships, 1876.

Section 6

William C. McMillan, Lot 12. Owner of the original Pontchartrain Hotel.

Section 7

Alexander Blain, Sr., Lot 29. Landscape designer and superintendent of Elmwood Cemetery, 1875–1915.

Section 8

Victor Colliau, Lot 121. Invented the Colliau Cupola for more efficient copper-mining operations, 1884.

Section 10

Daniel G. McAlpine, Lot 8. Pilot of the excursion steamer *Tashmoo.*

Dr. Alexander Blain, Lot 15. Founded Jefferson Diagnostic Clinic, one of the first medical clinics in the country, 1911. Founded Alexander Blain Hospital, 1921. President of Wayne County Medical Society, Detroit Academy of Surgery, Michigan Horticultural Society, and Detroit Science Society. Founder and first president of Michigan Audubon Society.

Joseph Burger, Lot 168. Detroit police captain, 1872.

Thomas J. Hudson, Lot 136. Author of one of the best-selling books of the late 1800s, *The Law of Psychic Phenomena.*

Dr. Theodore A. McGraw, Sr., Lot 5. A founder and professor of surgery at the Detroit Medical College, 1869–85.

George Pierrot, Lot 15. Host of a local television travelogue series during the 1960s. His marker is carved from a rock from his favorite Canadian fishing hole.

Elbridge A. Scribner, Lot 199. Developed the flower clocks powered by running water, such as the one at Greenfield Village, 1850–1926.

Section 11

Dr. Edward Jenks, Lot 99. President of the Detroit Medical College. Early staff member of Harper Hospital, 1833–1903.

Louis Ott, Lot 111. Justice of the peace, 1905–30.

Emily G. Stevens, Lot 54. Pianist and Mariners Church organist throughout the early and mid-1900s.

Mark B. Stevens, Lot 54. Partner and treasurer of R. H. Fyfe and Company, world's largest retail shoe business, 1849–1918.

Appendix 1

Feathered Residents

A walk through Elmwood is a birdwatcher's delight. The rolling topography with pond and stream has offered a natural sanctuary for both migrating birds and those permanently in residence over the past century. The following list of Elmwood birds was compiled by the Detroit Audubon Society:

American black duck
American crow
American goldfinch
American kestrel
American woodcock
Black-capped chickadee
Blue heron (migratory)
Bluejay
Brown creeper
Canada goose (migratory)
Cedar waxwing
Common grackle
Common nighthawk
Dark-eyed junco
Downy woodpecker
Eastern screech owl
European starling
Hermit thrush
House sparrow
Killdeer
Mallard

Mourning dove
Northern cardinal
Northern flicker
Red-headed woodpecker
Red-tailed hawk
Red-winged blackbird
Ring-billed gull
Ring-necked pheasant
Robin
Rock dove
Ruby-crowned kinglet
Ruby-throated hummingbird
Rufous-sided towhee
Sharp-shinned hawk
Snowy egret (migratory)
Snowy owl (migratory)
Song sparrow
White-breasted nuthatch
White-crowned sparrow
White-throated sparrow
Wood duck (migratory)

Appendix 2

Elmwood's Arboretum

More than sixteen hundred trees and shrubs, representing seventy species, are planted in Elmwood and valued at two million dollars.

Acer platanoides, Norway maple
Acer rubrum, red maple
Acer saccharinum, silver maple
Acer saccharum, sugar maple
Aesculus hippocastanum, horse chestnut
Ailanthus altissima, tree of Heaven
Betula alba, European white birch
Catalpa bignonioides, common catalpa
Cercis canadensis, redbud
Chamaecyparis thyoides, Atlantic white cedar
Cladrastis lutea, yellowwood
Cornus drummondi, roughleaf dogwood
Crataegus, hawthorn
Fagus grandifolia, European beech
Fraxinus americana, white ash
Ginkgo biloba, ginkgo
Gleditsia triacanthos, honey locust
Gymnocladus dioica, coffee tree
Juglans cinerea, butternut
Juglans nigra, black walnut
Juniperus horizontalis, trailing juniper
Liquidambar styraciflua, sweetgum
Liriodendron tulipifera, tulip tree
Magnolia macrophylla, bigleaf magnolia
Morus rubra, red mulberry
Nyssa aquatica, tupelo

Picea abies, Norway spruce
Picea glauca, white spruce
Pinus australis, longleaf pine
Pinus resinosa, red pine
Pinus strobus, white pine
Pinus sylvestris, Scotch pine
Platanus occidentalis, sycamore
Populus balsamifera, balsam poplar
Populus deltoides, common cottonwood
Prunus americana, American plum
Prunus erotina, black cherry
Prunus virginiana, chokecherry
Pseudotsuga taxifolia, Douglas fir
Pyrus americana, American mountain ash
Pyrus communis, domestic pear
Pyrus coronaria, American crabapple
Quercus alba, white oak
Quercus palustris, pin oak
Quercus rubra, red oak
Robinia pseudo-acacia, black locust
Salix humilis, tall prairie willow
Taxus, yew
Tilia americana, American basswood
Tsuga canadensis, Eastern hemlock
Ulmus americana, American elm
Ulmus pumila, Siberian elm

Appendix 3

Death Symbols

The decorative art on Elmwood's monuments is the silent, secret language of Detroit ancestors. Here is what some of the common images represent.

Anchor: hope.
Broken or draped column: early death; grief.
Butterfly: resurrection.
Cross: resurrection.
Cypress: hope.
Doorway, gates ajar: the afterlife; a soul entering heaven.
Dove: resurrection; the Holy Spirit.
Female figure: sorrow; grief.
Flag: military.
Flowers: beauty; a rose signifies sinlessness; a lily stands for purity.
Grieving eagle: military.
Gun: military service.
Hands clasped: farewell, or hope of meeting in eternity.
Helmet: military service.
IHS: eternity (Christian symbol; in English-speaking Christian tradition, "In His Service"; letters often incorporated in the Celtic cross).
Lamb: resurrection; a child.
Laurel leaves: victory.
Rising sun: resurrection.
Rope circle: eternity.
Shattered urn: old age.
Sheaf of wheat: old age.
Sleeping cherub: a child.
Snake: resurrection.
Sword, broken sword, crossed swords: military (crossed swords indicate death in battle).
Upturned torch: life extinguished.
Willow tree: sorrow; grief.

Sources

Bradshaw, Cora. "Up from Slavery 'Lisette' Owned City Land." *Oakland Press,* Feb. 29, 1988.

Broughton, Jan. "Spirits of Detroit." *Detroit News Magazine,* Sept. 24, 1989, pp. 6–14.

Catlin, George B. *The Story of Detroit.* Detroit: *Detroit News,* 1926, 107, 133, 196–97, 271, 514.

Creecy, John. *Detroit Tribune,* Memorial Day, 1868.

Farmer, Silas. *The History of Detroit and Michigan.* Detroit, 1884, pp. 52–53.

Grimm, Joe. *Michigan Voices.* Detroit: Wayne State University Press, 1987, p. 39.

Hathaway, Charles S. *Detroit Illustrated.* Detroit: H. R. Page, 1889.

Ledyard, Henry. "Yesterday's Headlines." *Detroit Historical Society Newsletter,* February 1968.

Lewis, Ferris E. *Michigan Yesterday and Today.* Hillsdale Educational Publishers, 1956.

"Life of Zachariah Chandler." *Detroit Post and Publishers Tribune,* 1880.

Linden-Ward, Blanche. *Silent City on a Hill.* Columbus: Ohio State University Press, 1989.

Lochbiler, Don. *Detroit's Coming of Age, 1873–1973.* Detroit: Wayne State University Press, 1973, chapters 17, 52.

Moon, Elaine. *Detroit 1701–1976.* Detroit Bicentennial Commission, 1976.

Olmstead, Frederick Law. *Elmwood Cemetery Board of Trustees Report.* John Bournman & Sons Printers, 1895.

Osterberg, Bert G. "Two Hundred Fifty Years in America: A Black Family." Paper presented at the African World Festival, Detroit, Aug. 21–23, 1987.

Panati, Charles. *Extraordinary Endings of Practically Everything and Everybody.* New York: Harper & Row, 1989, chapter 2.

Quaife, M. M., and William White. *This Is Detroit.* Detroit: Wayne State University Press, 1951, p. 18.

Rosentreter, Roger L. "Presque Isle County." *Michigan History,* January 1990, pp. 8–10.

Sloan, David Charles. *The Last Great Necessity.* Baltimore: Johns Hopkins University Press, 1991.

Stark, George W. "Detroit's Historic Valley of Bloody Run." *Detroit News Pictorial,* June 25, 1950, pp. 12–13.

Stevens, Mark C. "Elmwood Cemetery." Unpublished, 1975.

Treloar, James. "If Elmwood Stones Could Speak, Here Are the Stories They Would Tell." *Detroit News Magazine,* Dec. 12, 1976.

Voelker, Donald W. "Joseph Campau, Detroit's Big Shot." *Michigan History,* July 1991, pp. 39–43.

———. "Michigan and Trumbull Before Baseball." *Michigan History,* July 1989, pp. 25–31.

———. "Robert Stuart: A Man Who Meant Business." *Michigan History,* September 1990, pp. 12–19.

Walker, Monroe. "Slave Was City's First Black Leader." *Detroit News,* Feb. 1, 1983, p. 1A.

Weil, Tom. *The Cemetery Book.* New York: Hippocrene Books, 1992.

Woodford, Arthur, and Frank B. Woodford. *All Our Yesterdays.* Detroit: Wayne State University Press, 1969.

Index

Titles in the
Great Lakes Books Series